LECTURES

TO

YOUNG WOMEN.

By WILLIAM G. ELIOT, Jr.

PASTOR OF THE CHURCH OF THE MESSIAH, ST. LOUIS.

Third Edition.

BOSTON:
CROSBY, NICHOLS, AND COMPANY.
NEW YORK:
CHARLES S. FRANCIS AND COMPANY.
1854.

CAMBRIDGE:
METCALF AND COMPANY, STEREOTYPERS AND PRINTERS.

CONTENTS.

INTRODUCTORY LECTURE.

INTRODUCTORY LECTURE.

AN APPEAL.

"Favor is deceitful and beauty is vain; but a woman that feareth the Lord, she shall be praised." — Prov. xxxi. 30.

My present discourse will be introductory to a series of sermons, upon the duties and responsibility of woman. It is an undertaking upon which I enter with diffidence and almost with reluctance; for I can hope to say nothing new and have no desire to afford mere entertainment. My desire is to do good to those who hear me, and especially to the young, by exciting them to more serious reflection than they are probably accustomed to bestow upon the common duties of life and their responsibility to God. My only hope of accomplishing this is by the expression of well-known truths, in a plain and simple manner.

But how far plain truth, plainly spoken, will be acceptable, no one can tell until he tries.

The years of girlhood and early womanhood are generally so bright, that the shadow of mature reflection scarcely falls upon them. The enjoyment of life is so fresh and sweet, that the serious responsibility which life imposes seldom engages the thoughts. The path of life is strewn with flowers, and if thorns sometimes appear, it is only those which grow upon the flowers themselves and are inseparable from their beauty. The days of the young maiden dwelling under a father's roof, with the kind protection of a mother's love, shielded by the proud affection of brothers who love her almost with jealous tenderness, glide onward, not without care, not without disappointment, not without tears, but with almost uninterrupted enjoyment. She feels herself to be loved by every one, and that those whom she loves take pride in pleasing her. Their kindness is lavished upon her in daily tokens of affection; she is everywhere met with smiles; her most trifling endeavors to please are successful; she is praised as being amiable, if willing to be happy. I know that she has trials which seem to her very great; but in after life she will look back upon those years, before the serious duties of life began, as we recall a pleasant dream. When her brow is saddened under the weight of cares from which the wife and mother never escape, of the anxieties to which the tenderness of woman's nature always makes her subject, she will think of those blessed days when her chief responsibility was in childlike obedience, in the performance of duties so light that they were little more than recreation, rewarded by the approving smile or checked by the gentle rebuke of love, until the remembrance fills the eye with tears and the heart almost with sadness.

Fond and bright days of youth, enjoyed but once; when we know nothing of the world's sins, and very little of its grief; when all our friendships are inseparable and our confidence without reserve; when the denial of a pleasure is the severest trial, and the path of duty so easily trodden that the sense of duty is scarcely felt; when we hear of the wickedness of the world, only as one who sits at the quiet, cheerful fireside hears the howling of the storm and thinks vaguely, but pitifully, of the wretches whom it destroys; — we do not prize them as we ought until they are past, until, perhaps, "the days come, in which we say, we have no pleasure in them." We do not know how perfectly beautiful is the cloudless sky, or the bright April day when the fleeting showers serve only to give greater freshness to the earth's new beauty, until the long-continued storms of winter come, and the heavens are obscured by clouds, and the sun itself looks down upon us with cold and cheerless light.

Yet I would not speak as those who regret the short continuance of spring. The summer, and the autumn, and the winter are each beautiful in its place. Childhood and youth, the years of maturity and advancing life, and also the declining years of old age, may become to us equally full of real enjoyment, if, as we advance in that certain progress, we keep the face still turned towards heaven and walk in companionship with God. Nay, the true enjoyment of life should continually become greater. As the ripened fruit is better than the beautiful promise of spring, although gathered under skies that are becoming more sober, and the threatening of chill winter is near; so are the mature enjoyments of middle and advancing life better than the laughter and frolic of earlier days. And as the winter itself, which shuts up the treasure-houses of the kindly earth, and, by the withdrawal of external allurements, turns our thoughts to the pleasures of the fireside and friendly intercourse, and gives us time for reflection, often becomes the happiest season of the year; and we look forward with joy to its long evenings, in which, after the short day's duties are done, we learn how much we love each other, and the seclusion from the world makes our love more tender; so that there is no other season which we would so unwillingly spare, as that which at first seems the most dreary: Thus it is, in the experience of human life, that in its closing years, when the almond-tree begins to flourish, our highest and most perfect enjoyment may come. If the former seasons have been wisely spent; if we have laid up for ourselves a treasury of pleasant recollections, if the chambers of our imagery are filled with beautiful pictures; if, as we sit down quietly in the soberness of thought, the past brings no feeling of shame and the future no trembling; — then does that part of life, which seems to the observer so quiet as to be almost sad, become more excellent than all that has gone before. The step must lose its elasticity, but the heart may retain its youth. To the physical frame the grasshopper may become a burden, but the soul is stronger than in the days of youth, and all the burdens of time are light to him whose spirit reaches forward to eternity. I know how many are the sorrows of life; I know how poignant its grief, how severe its disappointments; but they who learn to remember the Creator in the days of their youth, and who walk with their Saviour as with a friend, going about to do good, consecrating their best strength to the service of God, will find that they daily become happy in the enjoyment of what God gives, and that the shadow which memory casts cannot obscure the brightness of that hope which shines upon their path from heaven.

But whence cometh this blessedness? The seed must be sown in spring, in the soft ground and under the fertilizing showers, the long days of summer must ripen it, while the weeds are kept away by careful cultivation, or the autumn will have no good fruit, and the needful provision for winter will be wanting. Those bright days of youth, when the heart is tender and smiles and tears so quickly chase each other, must have their hours of reflection and sober thought. The good seeds of virtue and religion must be then planted. We must cultivate them, with the hope that, under the dews of God's grace and the sunshine of his love, they may spring up and bear the fruit of righteousness, or our life will be a growing sadness; each added year will be an increasing burden, and sorrow will become the portion of our cup. We would not lessen the brightness of the maiden's life; the overflow of her innocent mirth brings gladness even to the heart of age. But she, too, should have her seasons of thought, of serious reflection and of prayer. Life is to her, also, a responsibility, a time of probation. She, too, has a duty to perform, and hereafter an account to render. She should learn to look, therefore, upon the earnest realities of life, not less than upon its brightness and beauty. She must not suppose, because she is so fondly cherished now, her wishes all consulted, and her pathway strewn with flowers, that it will always be so. The charms of beauty and youth may now secure the tokens of willing approbation, and the fondness of admiring hearts; but when these fade, as they must soon, unless their place is supplied by the better charms of a sweet temper, a well-educated mind, and a religious character, the neglect she will experience must be in the same proportion, both sad and humiliating. From this the chief disappointments of woman's life proceed. When her early fascinations surround her, she hears continually the language of praise; her faults are quickly excused, every hand is extended to help her, every face meets her with a smile. She supposes that it will always be the same, and so perhaps it would be if the same fascinations continued. But they must fade, and if nothing better takes their place, ought she to wonder if she is slighted, and the tokens of that spontaneous approbation withdrawn? Ought she not to have the good sense to perceive, that admiration is a different thing from love; and while she is pleased with the attention that youth and beauty bring, is it not better to seek for the affection which is founded upon respect? But who can respect the butterfly, however beautiful it may seem, however brightly clothed in the gay painting of its rainbow wings? Who wishes for, or can endure, as the companion of life, one whose highest thought is her own gratification, and by whom the incense of admiration is exacted as her unquestioned right?

It is pleasant for a time to expend one's ingenuity in the adornment of a beautiful image, or in gazing upon a beautiful picture; but who wishes to spend his life in such a way? Even if the image retain its beauty, and the picture the brightness of its hues, the language of admiration will gradually become faint, and more substantial pleasure will be sought. But if, as the truth must be, the fair image itself gradually loses its beauty, and the bright colors of the picture fade; if the sparkling diamonds, which we wreathe around the brow, begin to suggest the feeling of painful contrast, and the pearls encircling the neck serve only to call attention to the changes by which time marks his relentless steps, — who can wonder that weariness comes in the place of ecstasy, and sometimes disgust in the place of admiration?

I would not speak unkindly. I know how great are the wrongs which woman endures. There are shallow-hearted men enough, and selfish and bad men, under whose power, in the different relations of life, woman is placed.

They seek her love as a transient gratification to themselves, and when they have obtained it, use their power to disappoint all her hopes, to blight all her affections. They admire her at first only as the child admires a plaything, and, as the child, quickly become tired of it. They have not largeness of heart enough to appreciate the excellences of her character or to overlook the faults of her inexperience, and she becomes their servant through her whole life, in the vain endeavor to please those who are not worth pleasing, and to gain the love of those whom she has honored by loving. This experience is so common and so painful, that I cannot help wondering to see the readiness, almost the thoughtlessness, with which women trust the whole happiness of their lives to men of whom they know nothing, except that they are ingenious in paying compliments and persevering in their attentions. In return for this cheap incense, they bestow the best affection of their hearts, and lay up for themselves a store of disappointment. When the real trials of life and its vexations come, they find but little sympathy. Every thing that goes wrong is imputed to them; their silent but diligent exertion to make every thing go right, is unobserved; and life, instead of being the rich experience of mutual affection and forbearance and gentleness, one towards another, becomes almost a blank; — a routine of duty which brings no pleasure but that which the performance of duty always brings, and which wants that best human reward, the approbation of those we love.

Sometimes the case is still worse, and we see those who are gentle, pure-minded, and lovely giving their hands, with their hearts in them, to men who perhaps warmly love them in return, but whose habits and associations in life are well known to be such that a pure-minded woman ought to shrink from them, if not with horror, yet with distrust. They who incur such a risk are generally actuated, either by a degree of affection which prevents them from seeing the uncertainty, not to say the hopelessness, of the prospect; or by the romantic yet admirable spirit of self-sacrifice, which leads them to incur the most fearful danger, for the sake of saving those whom they love from ruin. They hope that their influence will be greater after marriage than before, and too often find, with breaking hearts, that it is less. They find, when too late, that their self-sacrificing devotion was misplaced, and that the martyr-spirit has not brought to them the martyr's reward. A noble effort indeed, a noble purpose, which none but woman's heart is able to conceive, but which even woman's love is seldom able to accomplish! If her influence over the man she loves is not strong enough to turn him from dissipated or sinful habits before she surrenders her liberty to him, there is little probability of such a result afterward.

If the possession of a virtuous woman's love, and the hope that she may become his own, is not enough to keep his hand from the cup of intoxication, and his feet from the paths where sinners walk, the claims of married life are not likely to do it. He will hear words of counsel from his betrothed, which he will not listen to from his wife. With the hope of bliss before him, he will make promises in which he fully believes, but which, having obtained his reward, he is not able to keep. I have had many opportunities of observing where this experiment has been tried, and the result has been so uniformly the same, that I am willing to run the risk of seeming harsh in its statement. My advice to a sister or to a daughter, and therefore to all whom I have the right to advise, would be given without any hesitation, without any reserve: "Be sure that the man whom you love is *now* a good and temperate and faithful man, or let your heart break, rather than become his wife. Say not to him, Conduct yourself rightly for six months, or twelve months, as a test of sincerity. It is insufficient. For so short a time and with so great reward in immediate prospect, a man must be brutal indeed not to restrain himself. But satisfy yourself beyond all reasonable doubt, that the principle of self-control is there, the practised love of virtue, the confirmed habit of a sober and pure life, before you speak another word of encouragement, and if possible before your love itself is bestowed."

I know that this language may seem too stern and rigid, but it does not come from stern or harsh feeling. There have been times when I have advised differently, but the result has taught me better.

She who becomes the wife of a man who has ever been dissipated, is incurring as great a risk as any one should incur, and far greater than she knows. Surely it is not too much to ask that the reform should be complete, unconditional, and long continued, before she trusts to its completeness.

But on the other side, if a woman has a right to demand the fixed character of a virtuous life, we too have a right to demand something. The man who discovers, when too late, that she whom he had pictured to himself almost as an angel, gentle, sweet-tempered, easily pleased, with a smile for every one and a frown for none, appeared so beautiful only because untried, — that her character has no depth, and her mind no real accomplishments, — is not to be blamed if he feels disappointed, nor to be wondered at if he shows his disappointment by neglect. He feels almost as if he had been entrapped, when he was entranced; that he has been betrayed into a foolish step by false appearances. Instead of finding a help-meet, he finds one who expects continually to be waited on, caressed, and flattered; who has no definite expectation except to spend the money which he makes, and to remain the idol of his affections because she consents to be admired.

On her part, she discovers her mistake soon enough, and, if she has moderately good sense, will studiously endeavor to increase the fascination of her character, as the charm of novelty dies away. But on his part the effect is too often a disenchantment which opens his eyes, even too widely, to her faults, and makes him impatient of her efforts to correct them. It is very hard for her to do after marriage what she ought to have done before; and it is a vexation to him to learn, that the whole substantial education of his wife is yet to be begun. Mutual disappointment brings mutual fault-finding, and the bliss of married life is found to have been a dream. If there is a general good purpose on both sides, and strong mutual affection, the lapse of two or three years will bring things right, with a comfortable degree of rational bliss. But it would be far better, if greater maturity of character could exist from the first. It would be far better, if those early disappointments and recriminations could be avoided, and this would be done, in part at least, if the self-education of woman in her youthful days were more carefully attended to; if it could be more deeply impressed upon her, that the graces of character are more excellent than personal loveliness, however attractive it may be.

The beautiful face attracts admiration, its pleasant smile wins the love, and all the surroundings with which youth and beauty encircle themselves dazzle the eye and take the heart captive. But she is very unwise who relies upon such things for her permanent influence, or as the foundation of happiness. It is those virtues which entitle her to be called lovely, and that cultivation of mind which enables her to share the thoughts and cares of her husband, while they command his respect, — it is these upon which she ought chiefly to rely. These do not come of themselves; they are the result of self-discipline, self-denial, and self-control. They are not obtained easily, but are partly the reward of persevering endeavor, and partly the answer to prayer.

I am inclined to think that young persons of the gentler sex give but little time to serious reflection, or to preparation for the real duties of life. The world in which they live is, in some respects, quite unreal and different from that upon which they afterwards must enter. The task of self-discipline and of self-education, both moral and religious, is more difficult because its necessity is less evident. The temptations to which they are exposed are few, the faults which they are likely to commit comparatively trifling, and their character is not so much in danger of being bad as of being unformed.

The young man, from the time of his first entrance into life, meets with the real trials and is exposed to the worst dangers of the world. The temptations which assail him are such, that if he yields to them he is manifestly ruined. The faults of which he is most likely to be guilty are in themselves sins and vices by the greatness of which his vigilance is kept alive. He feels it to be a question of life and death, and if he is wise, lays hold upon it as upon the work of salvation. The greatness and urgency of his work therefore nerve him to its accomplishment. Many fail to do it and are ruined, but by many it is faithfully accomplished, as I trust it will be by all those who may hear me this day.

But with woman the case is different. In the departments of life where those who now hear me walk, the question is not of virtue or vice, of sobriety or intemperance, of honesty or fraud. That question is settled by the circumstances of life and the restraints of society. She shrinks with horror from the world's iniquities, of which she knows almost nothing, and to which her thoughts are seldom turned. Let it be so always. Let there still be a part of the human family, from whose eyes human deformity is veiled. Let it be woman's privilege, not only to be free from the contagion of the world's iniquity, but to be ignorant, except so far as her own safety requires the knowledge, of its existence.

But does it follow that she has no faults to correct or to avoid? Are there no wrong tendencies of character, because they are likely to be checked before they reach their worst development? Such is not the estimate of sin given by the Gospel. It teaches us to measure the degree of guilt in every heart by the degree of selfishness and worldliness, rather than by the grossness or refinement of the outward act. The character may become so selfish, and the heart so worldly, and the mind so frivolous, that both the capacity and desire for improvement are almost lost, in those whose manners are perfectly ladylike, and whose morals, according to the common idea of morality, are perfectly correct. For a long time the evil may not be discerned. They who have every thing they wish for, and to whom almost every one is willing to give way, may be completely selfish almost without knowing it themselves, and without showing their selfishness in a manner to give offence.

They to whom the occupation of life is nothing but enjoyment, may become worldly to such a degree as to drive out all thoughts of God and religion, except so far as the church may be a fashionable resort, without being suspected of an irreligious life. They to whom laughter and mirth are so becoming, and upon whose lips the words of serious conversation seem almost out of place, may be immersed in frivolous and idle pursuits, until they are incapable of loving any thing else, without danger of being called silly or heartless. And so it happens, not unfrequently, that many pass from the days of girlhood to those of womanly years, without maturity of character, and completely unprepared for the real duties of woman's life. The transition is very sudden, from the entire freedom from care, to a multitude of little vexations which try the temper, to the responsible duties of wife and mother, for which the whole strength of a mature character is required. Then, too often, she finds how much she has been mistaken in herself, and her friends find, with equal disappointment, how much they have been mistaken in her. She craves undivided attention, and not receiving it, is vexed and impatient. She expects uninterrupted enjoyment, and not finding it, is discontented and full of complaint. Her temper, which seems so gentle, is found to be quick and petulant; her disposition, which in the sunshine was so sweet, proves to be, under the common trials of life, harsh and sour. Her friendship is invaded by envy, her love is so exacting that it continually finds food for jealousy, and the result is, at the best, the very commonplace character of a worldly-minded and selfish woman, whom it is difficult to love, and impossible to respect. It is the natural result of a character unformed, and of a mind undisciplined in early life. It is the natural, and not the extreme, development of those selfish and worldly tendencies, which her early education, as frequently conducted, is most likely to create.

Let the young lady pause for a few moments, and with serious reflection ask herself, how large a part of her time is given to amusement or to the preparation for it, which is sometimes her only labor, and how small a part to any thing that could be called self-education and religious improvement. How large a part is given to the adornment of her person, and how small to the adornment of her mind. With how great eagerness she prepares herself for the ball-room and theatre, and with what languor for the church. What diligent care she takes that her steps may be rightly trained for the mazy and intricate and sometimes objectionable dance, and how thoughtless she is whether her feet are walking in the pathway of duty, of propriety, and religion. I cannot but think that many, who are not purposely living bad lives, would be improved by such reflection. They would discover, perhaps, that their lives, without being bad, may be exceedingly unprofitable. They will certainly see, that a life which is little else than a varied routine of idle pleasures, of trivial cares and useless occupations, is but a poor preparation for the duties of a Christian woman.

You know that my views upon such subjects do not incline to austerity. I can discern no sin in youthful gayety, or in that glad merriment of heart so natural to those who are free from care. We do not expect, nor desire, at the age of sixteen, the stillness and sobriety of threescore years. It would be both unnatural and unamiable. But we may, nevertheless, concede that a touch of little more seriousness, a gentle shade of reflection, improves the fairest face, and gives to the most eloquent eye greater persuasiveness. There must be beauty of mind shining through the features, or they soon become insipid and uninteresting. Still more, there must be religious principle, and the earnest effort to form the character in the heavenly graces, or the experience of after life will show that the laughter was like the crackling of thorns, and that childhood and youth, with all their merriment, are but vanity.

It should also be remembered, that the influence of woman is very great when she is young and beautiful. Although she is not herself exposed, as a general thing, to the danger of great iniquity, her influence is very great upon those in whose path the temptation lies. The standard of morality among men is, to a considerable extent, fixed by woman. There are few men who will not admit that their training, either in virtue or vice, has been to a great degree according to the female influences under which their early lives were passed.

In my lectures to young men, I said that it depends upon them to elevate the tone of public sentiment, and to advance the cause of public morality, in this city; that it is for them to say whether intemperance and other forms of sin shall continue to increase among us, or daily become less ; that the moral character of our young men is the moral character of our city, and that the one can be elevated only by elevating the other. I believe that this is strictly true ; but perhaps there is an influence behind that equally to be regarded. Our young men give character to the city, but who gives character to them? What plastic hand is moulding them for good or evil? At what shrine is their allegiance first offered, and whose is that persuasive voice which it is, humanly speaking, impossible for them to resist? Very often, before religion has placed its restraining hand upon them, before they have adopted any fixed principle of life, the direction to their whole lives is given by an influence which they have felt, although it was scarcely discerned. They may trace their salvation or their ruin, for this life and the life to come, perhaps to the smile of encouragement, or the gentle expression of reproof, with which their first step in folly was encountered. I would not willingly excite a smile upon a subject so serious, nor turn the solemnity of these great interests into the channel of merriment; but it has been so truly said that it may be seriously repeated, — there is little hope of reforming young men, and keeping them in the path of virtue, unless we begin by reforming young women, and teaching them to give their best influence to the cause of goodness and sobriety. "You may rely upon it," said a young man to me not long since, and he was one who had felt the influence of which he spoke, "you may rely upon it, that, if they mix the drink for us, we will not refuse to take it. If their lips first touch the glass, we are sure to drain it. If they evidently think us better company when our tongues are loosened by wine, and join in the laugh when we tell them of our follies, ministers may as well stop their preaching, unless they can go a step farther back, and begin at the right place." It is quaintly said, and has the air, at first, of being half ludicrous, half satirical; but I fear that it is more than half true. The influence of the young lady, and her consequent responsibility, is very great. That influence is often thrown on the side of immorality and irreligion, simply because she does not think of it at all.

We do not speak now of specific actions, by which she often throws temptation in the way of those who seek her favor, — by leading them into extravagance, or to frivolous amusements, to the waste of time, and to false ideas of respectability, — nor to the fascination which she sometimes throws around the first steps of intemperance. Such subjects will have their proper place in other lectures. We are speaking now of general influence, — the influence which she exerts by her real character, by her ideas upon religious and moral subjects expressed by words and conduct. Every woman, whose manners are at all attractive, is exerting such an influence wherever she goes, to a degree which it is impossible to estimate. In every circle she fixes a standard of morality, above which few men care to rise. Woman's perception of virtue is generally understood to be more nice than that of men; and what satisfies her is sure to meet with their approval, and, generally speaking, they will not come quite up to the mark. If she speaks lightly of religion, they will blaspheme it. If she is devoted to pleasure, they will enter into dissipation. If she is heartless, they will be unprincipled. If she treats temperance as a joke, they will regard intoxication as a pardonable fault. What I now say may be mortifying to the pride of men, but it is true. We seldom rise quite up to the standard of morality and religion which woman holds before us. We never rise above it. In this respect she is the lawgiver and we are the subjects. The only hope for the moral advancement of society, is to keep woman in the advance-guard. Let her point the way and lead it, and the right progress is secured.

But she must do it not by words only, but by actions. The influence must come, if at all, from her real character. Does she love virtue and goodness? Does she respect religion and seek to make it the law of her own life? Is she striving to conform her heart and her conduct to the divine law of Jesus Christ? Then will her natural influence be strong and availing on the right side. Otherwise, whatever her occasional words may be, and whatever degree of horror she may express against some great iniquity, or against some poor creature, whose first steps in folly were taken under her direction, but who is now by drunkenness made unfit for her refined society, her inconsistency will plainly appear, and men will see that it is not the iniquity which she condemns, so much as its vulgarity and grossness.

There is but one way for any of us to exert a true influence, and that is by being true and faithful in ourselves. Especially is this so with woman, because hypocrisy is unnatural to her, and her real feelings almost sure to appear.

Let this, therefore, be the reflection with which my present lecture concludes. The moral and religious interests of society are in the hands of woman, and the only way by which she can conduct men right, is to be right herself. For "favor is deceitful and beauty is vain, but a woman who feareth the Lord, she shall be praised."

LECTURE II.

HOME.

"She looketh well to the ways of her household, and eateth not the bread of idleness." — Prov. xxxi. 27.

MY subject this evening leads us to the inquiry, What is woman's appropriate sphere of action, and the duties which chiefly devolve upon her?

Far be it from me, however, to enter upon those difficult and learned discussions concerning woman's rights and woman's mission, in which so many pens and tongues have been employed in modern times. These are subjects, I think, that offer little room for difference of opinion, except when misunderstood or improperly treated. Narrow-minded men and visionary women assume extreme positions, and arrogance on one side, and unreasonable demands on the other, are the result. On the one side it is assumed, with a self-sufficiency which would be provoking if it were not amusing, that the sum and substance of humanity is in the male branch of it, and that the female branch is only an afterthought, a needful circumstance in the case. On the other, the champion of woman contends that she will never have her full rights, until she is educated in every respect as man is, and shares every department of life with him, from the hall of legislation to the nursery inclusive. One is as far from right as the other, and both are equally unjust.

We do not wonder at the complaints of sensible women at the narrow limits assigned to their education. If they express the desire to know something more than school-books can teach, and to enter upon the fair domains of literature or the severer studies of science, they are greeted with some foolish sneer, or ridiculed as "strong-minded women"; as though there were something monstrous in a woman's cultivating her mind or finding delight in knowledge. When the sneer comes, as it generally does, from men who are themselves ignorant and superficial, as well as ill-mannered, it is pitiful, not less than ungenerous. But in recent times woman has sufficiently vindicated both her right and ability to enter into competition, wherever she pleases, in the department of prose or poetry, of science or philanthropy, with the wisest and best-educated men. They who speak the language of Miss Edgeworth and Joanna Bailey, of Mrs. Hemans and Mrs. Somerville, of Miss Sedgwick and Miss Dix, should never suffer one word of disrespect to pass their lips towards woman. Our current literature is adorned by her pen, our works of philanthropy are dependent, to a great extent, upon her sympathy and direct coöperation. She need, therefore, have nothing to fear from the comparison between her intellect and that of man; but it is a comparison between things unlike, and each of them is better than the other, in its own place. Let both be faithfully turned to the performance of those duties which, under the providence of God, devolve upon them, and no room will be left for the question, "Which is the greater?"

But leaving such unprofitable discussions, it will be admitted by all sensible persons, of either sex, that woman's best sphere of action and of influence is found, not abroad, but at home; not in the world at large, but in the bosom of her own family. Her own household is the kingdom in which, with her mild sceptre, she best reigns. She may indeed go out beyond it, but only as the missionary goes out from his own land to seek a field of labor less pleasant, less congenial to his taste. It constitutes the exception to the ordinary routine of her life, and in general all that she can elsewhere do is nothing, compared with her home influence and her home labors.

If all women performed their part in that small but noble sphere, there would scarcely be any work in the departments of morality and religion left undone. It is a sphere in which every woman can labor with success, and with the majority it is the only one in which success and happiness can be at the same time secured. Whatever may be woman's capacity for other departments of life, her taste, her sympathies, her affections, lead her to seek her own happiness and usefulness in the circle of her friends and kindred, under her father's or husband's roof, rather than in the larger but more superficial relations of the world. And we may further add, that, whatever may be her success elsewhere, and however useful she may become, she is seldom an object worthy of admiration, unless in her home influence she is also blessed. The woman who neglects her home, who abstracts therefrom her first affections, her dearest interest, her most earnest efforts, is sacrificing more than she can gain, except under very extraordinary circumstances. She will probably sacrifice her own happiness and that of all whom she ought most to love.

Superficial persons may think that this is a contracted view of woman's sphere and duties. To confine her chiefly to the four walls of a house, and to limit her influence to a family of five or six persons, is like burying her, and is thought to be great social injustice.

Why may she not have the whole great sphere of the world to act in? Why should her influence be more limited than that of man? We answer, that our real influence is often stronger, for being limited in its immediate action. The wider diffusion of our efforts lessens their strength, and sometimes prevents their efficacy. The greatest heat, for practical purposes, is produced by an instrument which concentrates the flame upon a single point. The hardest metals then cannot resist its power. But the same heat, diffused a very little, is of no avail. And so do we often see that the concentrated influence of affection is strong enough, in the sacred precincts of the family relation, to melt away the dross from the most stubborn heart, and shape the heart itself after the heavenly pattern, when all influences out of doors, and all the discipline of common life, have had no effect.

Again: it must be remembered that home influence extends beyond home. The best way to purify a stream is to cleanse its fountains, and less effort will accomplish the work if begun there. The great current of society is created by those thousand little streams, which are pure or impure according to the character of our homes. To purify them, or to keep them pure, is chiefly woman's work; and if truly done, the current would roll on, pure as a mountain stream, to the eternal ocean. If it be not well done, all the Howards and Wilberforces can only succeed in filtering, here and there, a little of the corrupted water.

So true is this, that the strongest and most enduring influence which any of us exert, is that which begins at home, and goes out widening and deepening into the world. Whether men or women, the day of judgment will probably show this to be true. A celebrated preacher once said, that the most successful sermon he ever preached was to an audience of one person, on a very stormy day. That one person was converted and became the instrument of doing good to thousands. The mother has an audience of five or six, to whom her life preaches, and if she can have the blessing of God to convert them from sin to holiness, from the world to God, she accomplishes a work which God only can measure. I doubt if any woman, who devotes herself, both mind and heart, to its accomplishment, would call the sphere ignoble or the work insignificant. It seems so only to those who have not heart enough to appreciate it rightly, or mind enough to understand its greatness; and they will waste themselves in peevish complaint, because they have not a wider sphere of action, when the real difficulty is, that they are incompetent to the work which God has already given them to do. I know many who are unfit for this home duty, none who are degraded by it. The reason why there is so much left for philanthropists to do, is this, — that home work is done so badly. The great primal reform is needed there, and will never be accomplished until woman does it. The man may help her or hinder; but however loudly he may call himself the head of the family, she is the heart; and it is the heart which creates the life-blood and diffuses it through the whole system.

There is an unworthy estimate of home and home-life, which values it only for its physical comforts, and under which my language would be extravagant. Some men think of it only as a more convenient and pleasant way of living than is found in hotels or eating-houses; and according to their view, woman is little more than a cooking and mending animal, a kind of upper servant, sometimes with reduced wages, whose duty is to provide for the wants of her lord and master and take good care of his children. Perhaps we should say that some men used to think thus; for such opinions are now generally discarded or acknowledged to be very coarse. Yet they are not quite out of date, and occasionally you will hear the vulgarism of the great Napoleon applauded, that "she is the most eminent woman who has had the most children," or the equal vulgarism of a less man, that the most important question as to a woman's education is, whether she can prepare a good dinner, or mend an old garment;—questions which, if made the most important, indicate that we put the same estimate upon eating with the glutton, and upon economy with the miser.

But on the other hand, we must not undervalue the humble details of household care, which occupy so much of woman's time, the world over.

A great part of the comfort and happiness, and therefore of the good social influence of home, depends upon the manner in which these trifling details are attended to. A slovenly house, or a badly ordered table, or ill-clothed children, make an uncomfortable home, and a man must be a saint to resist its unhappy influence on his character. Just as it is the man's duty to provide a home for his family, and to supply it with conveniences according to his means, it is woman's duty to adorn it with the excellent graces of good taste, and either by her own industry or the well-directed industry of those who serve her, to fill it with the healthful influences of cleanliness, good order, and neatness; so that every thing may minister to the comfort and enjoyment of those she loves. From these duties nothing can excuse her, except the disability of sickness. For their omission, no excellences in other things can compensate. She may not neglect them, even to find time for study or reading, in the improvement of her mind; not even for works of philanthropy or in relieving the poor; much less for idle gossiping or visits of etiquette, or the perusal of the last novel. We care not how high she may be in her social standing, nor how humble her lot; if she has a home, whether it be a palace or a single room, the ordering of her own household, with all its trifling occupations, is her first duty and should be her first care. Without it, her home influence, and therefore her chief influence, is lost.

But while we rate such humble duties at their highest value, considered as means to a spiritual end, we say that the man who prizes woman chiefly because she is capable of performing these and similar tasks, does not deserve to have a good wife. He should merely employ a housekeeper and pay her good wages. And the woman whose idea of duty stops here, whose highest ambition is to keep house well, has but very low conceptions of her proper dignity, and is unworthy to be the wife of a sensible man. There are social, moral, and spiritual uses, proceeding from the wise regulation of the household, which bestow dignity on what would otherwise be trifling, and give value to things which would otherwise serve only to please the taste or gratify the senses. The pleasantness and comfort of home is the machinery with which woman works, if she well understands her office, for the education of the heart, for purifying the character, of each member of her family. It is thus she shuts out the temptations of the world. It is thus that she teaches her husband and her children to depend on the quiet enjoyments of the fireside, which elevate while they refresh. Her home is her Garden of

Eden, or she has none, and she knows that the more carefully the flowers are cultivated and the fruit ripened, not only the more beautiful, but the more healthful both for mind and body, will it be. She thus expresses her gratitude to God from whom her blessings proceed, and her affection to her friends and kindred, for whose happiness her mind is continually watchful, and on whose behalf she makes a hundred sacrifices, so unpretending that they are often unobserved, — but not the sweetness of temper from which they proceed, while she seeks her own best delight in the enjoyment of others. With a spirit like this no occupation is trifling, no duty insignificant. The educated woman sometimes complains of the petty nature of her cares and the increasing perplexity of trivial things; but let her mind be elevated, let her have a noble ultimate design, and you change every thing. Give her that spirit in the service of God, by which we live above the world while we live in it, and by which she can look through all the vexations that annoy her, to the hearts of those for whose happiness her care is expended, and you impart beauty to the most ordinary routine of her life; to the humblest domestic duties which poverty or the unreasonable exactions of unreasonable men can lay upon her. Under such circumstances we may sometimes regard her, though busied in what seem menial labors, with feelings little short of reverence.

Go into the poor man's house, when he is at his hard toil in the world, and witness the patient, uncomplaining industry of his wife, who seems to forget that she has wants of her own, in her busy zeal to supply the wants of others, and in whose eye the unbidden tear rises when, at his return home, she is greeted with no word of praise or kindness; for which she excuses him in her heart, because he is tired in body and anxious in mind. Or look upon the widow upon whom has devolved the labor of supporting and educating her children, as she sits almost unmoving from early morn far into the hours of night, plying that little instrument, her needle, until her eyes ache and

4

her fingers are stiff, and yet her heart is buoyant with gratitude to God, because she can find work to do; and I think we shall be able to understand that the sphere in which their souls work is greater, in proportion as the labor of their hands seems less.

It requires a great heart to turn small things to heavenly uses. The cup of cold water given to the thirsty, in the name of Jesus Christ, becomes a heavenly work and obtains the approval of the Heavenly Father. It is not what we do, outwardly considered, but the spirit in which it is done, that constitutes the greatness or littleness of our work. The details of all our lives are insignificant, and in this respect few have a right to boast over the rest. The merchant, the farmer, the mechanic, the lawyer, spend three fourths of their time in labors which are respectable only because of the object in view. Men sometimes speak contemptuously of woman's work, forgetting how much their happiness depends upon its faithful discharge; and women are too apt to admit that their employments are unimportant, compared with those of men. But, for myself, as a careful observer of both, I cannot perceive why woman, who is working with a smile that bestows a charm on the plainest occupation, ingeniously contriving to make a little go a great way, and of small means obtaining great comfort, is not employed in work quite as dignified as trading for sugar and coffee, or the selling of cotton and woollen goods, or the chaffering about freights and exchanges. From the way in which men sometimes talk, you would suppose that dollars and cents are the only respectable thing in the universe; that successful speculation is the only true heroism, and that the hope of making twenty per cent. profit is enough to bestow dignity upon meanness itself. But careful thought will show us, that our comfort, our happiness, our improvement, our general well-being, depend more upon what is called woman's work than upon man's. They depend, not so much on the success of our counting-rooms and workshops, and a good balance-sheet at the end of the year, as upon the judicious management and skilful ordering of domestic life. We may be happy with a very small income, if the home department is so managed that every thing is used to the best advantage, and good taste made to supply the place of luxuries; and there will still be something left, out of what would otherwise have been wasted, for the poor. But who can be contented in a house, where style is substituted for neatness, and large expenditure brings little comfort, and the idleness of the inmates gives abundant time for fretfulness? We can educate our children to be useful and happy, however poor we may be; but not in a household which witnesses daily contention and complaining, where frivolous amusement is made to take the place of rational enjoyment, where the influence of the mother fails to commend virtue and religion to her sons and daughters.

We would not imply that every thing in the home depends upon the female members of it. Some men are so selfish or depraved, so ill-natured and petulant, so unreasonable in their expectations, and so thankless when they have no room to be dissatisfied, that, if they were to find angels at home, they would contrive, by their own presence, to prevent them from an angel's bliss. But we speak in general terms when we say, that, in civilized Christian communities, the praise of well-directed families and the blame of disorderly ones belong chiefly to the woman. Let man be ever so wise in his own conceit, the credit chiefly belongs to her; let her be ever so ingenious in excuses and in throwing the fault from herself upon the circumstances by which she is surrounded, to herself principally may the fault be traced. That exceptions exist, we know, but what we have now said is, generally speaking, true.

We desire to magnify, although we cannot exaggerate, the importance of the institution of home. The more so, because this is the best means of elevating woman in the scale of social life, to the point which belongs to her of right, but has not yet, in any part of the world, been fully conceded. In this country, every thing depends upon it. It is the nursery of republican simplicity and republican virtue. It is the wholesome restraint upon our eagerness, the conservative influence which prevents radicalism from excess; an influence stronger than patriotism and from which the purest patriotism springs. It binds us to the love of peace. It counteracts the angry feelings of political contention and the conflicting interests of different parties. Destroy it, or our love for it; make this whole nation an out-of-door people; teach them to find their amusement, their happiness, away from home, in gardens, in *cafés*, in the streets, as it is in France and Italy, — and it would be as difficult to maintain our republic, as it has been to establish one in Paris or Rome. No one who has ever visited those cities, or Naples, or Venice, or who has studied the habits and customs of their population, can fail to see the cause of their violent commotions, and uneasy, restless striving. The mass of the people are without homes and home influences. They live out of doors, in perpetual excitement, and the only idea of home to thousands of them is a place to sleep in. By this means, woman is, for the great part, shut out from her proper influence on society. She is deprived of her rightful working-place, and cannot work to good advantage. She becomes the drudge, or the toy and plaything, or at best the ornament of society, instead of being the messenger of truth, the guardian of virtue, the angel of mercy.

The foundation of our free institutions is in our love, as a people, for our homes. The strength of our country is found, not in the declaration that all men are free and equal, but in the quiet influence of the fireside, the bonds which unite together the family circle. The corner-stone of our republic is the hearth-stone. Therefore let men see that it is carefully laid; let woman's hand keep it clean and bright; around it let happy faces gather and happy hearts beat in gratitude to God. From the corroding cares of business, from the hard toil and frequent disappointments of the day, men retreat to the bosom of their families, and there, in the midst of that sweet society of wife and children and friends, receive a rich reward for their industry, and are reminded that their best interests are inseparable from public and social morality. How different would it be, if, instead of this, he turned to the resorts of public pleasure, to the partisan debates of political clubs, or any other organization from which woman's influence is excluded, for the refreshment of his mind and body. The merry talking of children's voices is a more eloquent persuasive to virtue and patriotism, than the speeches of orators or demagogues. The feeling that here, in one little spot, his best enjoyments are all concentrated, made pure through being shared with female purity; the consciousness of dependence, through the strong affections of his heart, upon those who for protection and support depend upon him; his almost unconscious yielding to the gentler influence of one who is second to him, only because her good sense yields the precedence; — all this gives a wholesome tendency to his thoughts, and is like the healing oil poured upon the wounds and bruises of the spirit.

Nor is it a fancy picture which we have now drawn. In ten thousands of homes, each day, at set of sun, in every part of our happy land, are these strong but quiet influences at work. In every one, woman is proving herself a true philanthropist, a conservator of public order, the promoter of social harmony. While she does this work faithfully, — although Providence may open a wider sphere of action, under the revolutions of modern society, — she cannot have a nobler sphere, nor one wherein she can be more useful or more happy.

We know that different scenes are often exhibited. Uniformly our best blessings may be abused to become the worst evils. It is not every roof-tree under which we may sit, with none to molest or make us afraid. It is not every woman who knows how to make home pleasant. Something more is requisite than boarding-school accomplishments and a milk-and-water character; something more than an education in a female college, with the degree of Mistress of Arts. There are houses enough, in which woman is content to be little better than a doll to wear finery or a child to be amused; and there are others, in which sufficient proof is given of Solomon's words, that "a continual dropping in a very rainy day and a contentious woman are alike."

But still, after all exceptions have been made, in our homes is our chief strength. There is our best happiness as a people. There the strongest influences in favor of virtue and religion are at work. They are the school-houses, in comparison with which all other schools and colleges, both public and private, are of no importance, and in them is woman's place and woman's work. The Emperor of the French said, which is a partial offset to his absurd saying already quoted, that the chief necessity in reforming the system of national education was well-educated mothers. With equal force may it be said that the prosperity of our land, the permanence of our institutions, can be secured only through the influence, which must be the home influence, of sensible and virtuous women. Legislators are good in their place, but for our happiness and virtue as a people, we must depend upon that legislation which is spoken in the gentle voice, so excellent a thing in woman; urged by the pleadings of woman's love, enforced by the penalties of woman's displeasure.

If the views now presented are correct, we do not degrade woman by teaching that home is her rightful place, the sphere of her chief influence. If she has a heart large enough and a mind sufficiently educated to perform her duties there, looking well to the ways of her household and eating not the bread of idleness, she is the equal of any man, however great or good or wise he may be. She is his equal in position, his equal in practical usefulness.

But we have reason to fear that the views now presented are not sufficiently regarded. Home is not made so sacred a place as it ought to be. Its influence is not exclusively given to the cause of temperance and righteousness. Even where its general influences are good, frequent and melancholy exceptions are made, by conforming to wrong usages and the continuance of foolish customs. When the festive board is spread and all the refinements of woman's skill have been exhausted to make it attractive, its crowning glory is found in the wine "which moveth itself aright, but at last stingeth like a serpent and biteth like an adder." Her hand becomes ingenious to fill the sparkling bowl, and her encouragement is given to those "that tarry long at the wine, who rise up early in the morning that they may follow strong drink, that continue until night till wine inflame them." I would not go beyond the limits of propriety, to interfere with the social arrangements prevalent among us. Every person claims the right of directing the affairs of his own family, and of receiving his friends according to his own ideas of hospitality. I do not dispute the right, but wish it were exercised more discreetly. I am afraid that the strongest influence on the side of intemperance, and the hardest to overcome, is that of the social circle, the hospitable board. In our homes, which should be the centre of every good influence, that bad influence is at work. In every citadel of our safety, the most dangerous enemy gains free admission. It is there that the thoughtless habit which ends in dissipation is begun. There it finds encouragement, under all the appliances of luxury and elegance, until it shows itself in the unsteady step and reeling brain. I have known many young men to be betrayed into confirmed habits of intemperance, by their frequent acceptance of this well-intended kindness. There are probably those who will have been, this week and the next, intoxicated for the first time in their lives, because it is so difficult and awkward to refuse the reiterated invitations of woman's hospitality. Is it not particularly to be regretted, that Christmas day, the commemoration of the Saviour's birth, and the close of the year, which should call for reflection and repentance, and the beginning of the new year, which ought to be hallowed by virtuous resolutions, become to many the first step towards ruin? Can we not be hospitable in a less dangerous way? Can we not make our friends welcome without exposing them to danger? Is not the pleasant smile and the grasp of a friendly hand and the feast which cheers without inebriating, — are not these enough? If any require more, let them seek it where they may sell their virtue for a price. Let not woman's hand lead the way to temptation. Let not her pleasant home lend its attractions to the sins which so easily beset us.

Is there a mother who would place temptation in the way of her son? Is there a sister who would make virtue difficult to her brother? Is there a maiden who would place in the hand of him whom she is already beginning to love, the poison which may find, and perhaps has already begun to find, its way to his heart? Is there a wife who would surround her husband with snares, so skilfully covered that he may fall into them almost unawares? You may have the utmost confidence in those you love, as we all have; for love casteth out fear: but is it worth while to try experiments, when the stake at issue is so tremendous? We may be very sure that they are in no danger; but is it not well to remember that prayer, "Lead us not into temptation," and shall woman be the tempter? If not for the sake of those whom she herself loves, yet for the sake of those whom others love, let her refuse to become the minister of evil.

Those who are tempted may not be her own friends and kindred; she may look upon them with entire indifference, and offer the temptation only because custom requires it: but there are hearts beating sadly for those who yield; there are wives and mothers and sisters who will have reason to mourn over the day when the temptation was offered, and the custom which permitted it.

Nor is it only upon one day in the year, but frequently, almost as a needful part of hospitable entertainment, the subtle and almost irresistible attack is made upon the virtue of those who only desire an excuse for yielding. Festive assemblies which begin with all the splendor that wealth can purchase, and at which the beauty, the fashion, and the elegance of the city are gathered, sometimes end with scenes in the private parlor which would not be creditable to the public tavern. At such times even woman's eye sparkles with an unwonted fire, and the gayety of her merriment is something more than the natural flow of her own spirits. To the whole she lends her countenance; and her influence, as the presiding genius of the household, is given to that which in heart she despises and hates.

I have no expectation of changing general customs by my feeble voice. I know how tyrannical fashion is, and that there are many persons who would commit any sin or incur any danger sooner than be accounted unfashionable. "Custom lies upon us as a weight, heavy as frost," and not one in a hundred has the strength or courage to throw it off, though conscience may command and the safety of those whom he best loves require it. But the improbability of success is no reason for being silent. They who attempt nothing are quite sure to accomplish nothing. Social usages, like those to which I refer, can be more easily changed than we at first suppose. If a comparatively small number of those who are raised by their wealth and hospitality above the accusation of meanness, and by their standing above the suspicion, so dreadful to endure, of being unfashionable, — if a few of such families were to begin the change, there would be many to follow, and twelve months would show great and general improvement. The young would have reason to bless such a change, for one of their chief dangers would be removed. Still more would they have reason to bless it, who have once yielded to temptation and are now exerting themselves to resist. Too often have I seen those, who have held firmly to their resolution through a whole year, inadvertently betrayed into the ruin from which they had almost escaped, by the multiplied temptations which custom has prescribed.

And am I wrong in thinking that it is

woman's influence to which we must look for the change required? Do I overrate it, when I say that, if she really wishes for the change, it will be accomplished? There are undoubtedly some men so arbitrary and self-willed, that they will not be directed even by the gentlest hand and for their own good. But under the worst of circumstances she can moderate the evil and greatly diminish its allurements. Generally speaking, in well-regulated families, it is so far under her control, that what she heartily wishes she can easily accomplish.

I commend it, therefore, to your serious, may I not say to your religious attention. It is a serious subject, upon which the best interests of society depend. Do not treat such things as conventionalities, that must take their own course; for you have an influence to exert, a duty to perform, which cannot be neglected without sin. It is a duty which rests upon you as mothers, as wives, as sisters, as daughters, as friends: yes, as women. Not one of you can escape from it. If it were faithfully performed, if the influence were heartily exerted, I believe that the whole great question of temperance would be triumphantly carried. Men are not brutal enough to love intoxication, unless they learn to love it in woman's society. Their first step she can easily prevent; but afterwards, when she begins to loathe their presence, even her voice fails to call them back.

Let these things sink into our hearts. I have spoken of them, because I think they need to be spoken of. Their neglect will be our ruin. The necessity of a change is already felt, and before many years are past, many of these usages, now fashionable, will be accounted, not only dangerous, but vulgar. By adopting the right principle as our guide, let us go in advance of fashion, and do what we can to discountenance wrong customs. We may do it silently, or as quietly as you please; but let it be done decidedly, and it will be effectual. At least it will be the performance of our own duty, and a proof that we fear God more than we fear man.

It will make our homes the sanctuary of virtue, as they ought to be. "It must needs be that temptations come"; but to that assertion of the Saviour another is added, well calculated to startle us in view of our own accountability: "Woe unto them through whom the temptation cometh."

LECTURE III.

DUTIES.

"Her children rise up and call her blessed; her husband also, and he praiseth her."—Prov. xxxi. 28.

THE object of my last lecture was to show that the best interests of society are, to a great extent, in woman's keeping. In the departments of morality and religion, of refinement, of good taste, of philanthropy, of education, and of all the other great agencies of civilization, she has at least an equal share, both in the work to be done and the end to be accomplished. If men would frankly acknowledge this, it would elevate her more highly in their estimation. They would respect her more and pay more deference to her opinions; they would take more pains to give her the advantages of education, so as to secure the proper use of that influence which, either for good or evil, she is sure to possess. We fear that they are now more willing to pay the tribute of admiration than of respect. They regard her only as a being to be cherished and protected, and whose loveliness is never so great as when she leans upon them for support. They take pains to please her, very much as we try to please children; and she very often consents to be pleased with toys and playthings and flattering words and unmeaning phrases, with dress and equipage and jewelry and other trifles lavished upon her quite as much through worldly pride as from sincere affection. It may be all right in its way, nor do I speak now with a view to its condemnation; but when this kind of adulation, this money-bought worship, is the only or the best evidence of our respect, we are in fact contributing to degrade her whom, for our own amusement, we seem to exalt, and are treating her as a child whom we ought to treat as an equal.

It would be better if the adulation were less and the respect greater. She can dispense with the empty compliments, which men are skilful to use in proportion to the shallowness of their own brains, in consideration of receiving a more silent homage, the language of real esteem. We seldom compliment directly those whom we respect, and whenever we do so, it is with delicacy and hesitation, showing that we feel ourselves to be upon dangerous ground. The language of compliment is generally the language of superiority. We flatter those whom we think beneath us, and who will therefore be pleased by our notice and approval. Towards those who are above us, more deferential language and fewer words are used. Only when with our equals, whom we acknowledge to be such, do we offer and receive those expressions of cordial friendship and sympathy, which are more pleasant than any other form in which praise can come.

In the compliments which men pay so freely to the gentler sex, I am afraid that they give greater evidence of their own self-conceit and assumed superiority than of any thing else. I think, therefore, that if men would learn the real truth as to woman's influence, — that they themselves are moulded, in mind, in affections, in character, by woman's hand, — it would do them good, both by teaching a lesson of modesty, and by reminding them to be just before they talk so much of being generous.

On the other hand, it is equally important to woman herself to understand her true position. In civilized communities she is actually exerting an influence to which no limit can be placed. As I said in a former lecture, she is the lawgiver of social morality; she fixes the standard of right and wrong in social intercourse, according to which men shape their ideas, and to which they conform their practice. Individually she may seem very weak, but as a sex, in the different relations of life, she is all but omnipotent. No effort to advance society can succeed which does not begin with her and receive her coöperation. Whether it be temperance or charity, religion or education, the most essential thing is to excite her interest and give to her correct ideas, arousing her to a sense of duty and responsibility. When that is done, the battle is half gained, and what is more, it is the first half, and almost sure to be followed by complete triumph. If woman felt this, it would inspire her with greater self-respect; it would enable her to place its proper value on the flippant praise of which she is now sometimes so fond; to smile at the words of flattery, but not on him who uses them. She would feel herself entitled to higher respect than such words imply. She would feel the responsibility which so great influence imposes, and prepare herself, by self-education and religious self-discipline, for the duties which properly devolve upon her.

Let us look, then, more particularly at the different relations in real life which woman actually holds, and the important position in which she is placed. When we have done this, we shall be prepared to ask whether her education, as now generally conducted, is what it ought to be; and I think that the answer to this question will be more evident than satisfactory.

First, we speak of that sacred relation in which our love towards her is mingled with veneration; in which, while she is living, if we are wise, and certainly after she is dead, she becomes to our hearts almost as the saints in heaven, through our remembrance of her patient suffering, her unwearied love, her gentle, sad, yet hopeful rebukes; her pleading voice when we were wrong; her sympathy when we were tempted; her readiness to forgive when we committed sin; her encouragements when we tried to do right; her tenderness when she wiped away our tears; her gladness when she shared in our joys, — and all the nameless but unforgotten tokens of a Mother's love.

That is the gentlest, the sweetest word which falls from human lips. It speaks of a human relation, but mingles with religion itself. The great reason why the worship of the mother of Christ has obtained so strong possession of a large part of the Christian world, is this: that the word itself excites a yearning in the human heart, calling up its dearest associations, exciting its tenderest affections, and giving to men an opportunity of expressing, in religious homage, the feelings of gratitude, penitence, and filial love, which the name of mother never fails to excite. How much we owe to her, none can tell. The treasures of love which she has expended upon us, God only knows; for she herself is scarcely conscious how rich and inexhaustible they are. As she holds her infant smiling in her lap, her first-born, a new existence has begun to her. She watches the half-formed smile, and her own smile answers it. She catches the first ray of intelligence, from eyes which look wondering upon this strange world into which the heavenly visitant has entered, and gaze around uncertainly, without expression, until the beaming light of the mother's face is caught, and that first ray of conscious intelligence is but the reflection of the mother's love. From day to day, how carefully she guards him, and at night his gentlest movement arouses her to renewed watchfulness. His playfulness in health is her chief delight, and the distant approach of sickness fills her with dread. To say that she would die for him would be but little; she would die for him a thousand times, for the dearest charm in her own life is in the life of her child.

The image of God's providence is found in the mother's love. As he is good to the unthankful and the evil, so is her love never estranged by our utmost waywardness, by our worst desert. The love of an earthly father may sometimes be withdrawn, and the sternness of his nature may drive the sinful child from his presence, with words of anger almost like imprecation. He may pronounce a curse which drives the offender to despair. But the mother cannot curse; her love cannot be withdrawn. The sorrow of her child's guilt has pierced her heart, only to make it more tender; her hand seeks to draw him back, even when unwilling to return; her prayers are for him when he will not pray for himself; and upon her bosom he finds a resting-place, where he may again lay his weary head, as confidently as when he reposed it there in the unquestioning trust of infancy.

But if, escaping from the snares of sin and strengthened under the temptations of the world, her child grows up in the strength of virtue, in the purity of religion; if she sees her sons and daughters respected and useful and happy, by their affection endeavoring to return their mother's love and shield her from the harms so frequent to declining age; — then, who can tell the mother's joy, or the earnestness of her thanksgiving, except the God before whom she kneels in silent gratitude? That is indeed a blessing with which her cup runneth over. Her children are her pride, her joy, the jewels that circle her brow, the ornaments more becoming to her age than any other; and her face, although it may show the lines of advancing years, retains its youthfulness of expression and a smile more lovely than that of youth itself, when the names of her children are spoken with praise, and the record of their usefulness brought to her ears.

O, if we could but understand the depths of a mother's love, the complete disinterestedness of her strong affection, the days of our early life would be stained with fewer sins, and our memory in after days less heavily burdened. If we could but understand how heartless it is, for the sake of some transient pleasure, some worthless dissipation, for the indulgence of a whim or the gratification of ungoverned temper, to send the pang of grief to that loving heart, to bring the shade of mortification over that hopeful face, we should be more careful in our pleasures, more reluctant to do wrong. There is no method by which we can pay the debt of gratitude to her, except by lives which are an answer to her prayers for our sake. If she hears of our disappointments, she is sad; our sorrows and bereavements are hers, not less than our own; but these, as we are not able to escape from them, she is ready to receive as the discipline of God's providence, for her good and for ours. But our sins lie like a weight upon her soul. To our departure from God she cannot reconcile herself. That is a grief she scarcely knows how to bear, and under which her gray hairs are brought in sorrow to the grave. Let me appeal to you, to you who are young, for her sake. Let your thoughtlessness be checked, let your folly be stayed. If not for God's sake, nor for Christ's sake, yet for your mother's sake, hold back your hand from sin! Lay not up for yourselves that store of repentance which comes from the remembrance of a mother's grief, of a mother's unanswered prayers!

While I speak, we feel how great must be the influence of a mother's character upon us; that if she is a faithful woman, God-fearing and God-trusting, we become almost as wax in her hands, softened by the warmth of her love, moulded by her gentle touch, until we grow to the years of mature life, and find ourselves, in a great degree, what she has made us. We would not say absolutely that it depends upon her what her children shall be in time and in eternity, for that would be attributing to human strength more than it can properly claim. Our best skill and wisdom, even the influence of a good example, sometimes fail. Children who are educated under the most judicious system, and for whom no pains are spared, sometimes disappoint all our hopes; while those who are most neglected, and under the worst influences of bad example in their parents and of depravity in the world, are snatched like brands from the burning and grow up in piety and usefulness. We must not therefore feel that it depends upon us alone. We are not sufficient to ourselves in any thing, least of all in the performance of our duty as parents, and if there is any one on whom the command to pray without ceasing is especially enjoined, it is the Christian mother, when her children are around her. She cannot feel too strongly, in her family, the necessity of God's grace, guiding and protecting those she loves.

Moreover, in speaking of the mother's influence over her children, we must remember that her wisest efforts are sometimes defeated by influences which she cannot control. I have known instances in which the father has taken pains, even in their early childhood, to lead them in the paths of wickedness, to teach them contempt for religion, to repeat for their learning words of blasphemy, to carry them into bad company and to place them at six years old upon the counter of a bar-room to learn the first lesson of drunkenness. In such a case shall the mother be blamed for the fruitlessness of her efforts, or should we expect any thing but the ruin of her child? and even in cases less flagrant than this, a bad temper and tyrannical disposition will bring almost as bad results. The labor of directing her children and governing them is sometimes left exclusively to the mother, without any assistance from her husband, and is sometimes made almost hopeless by his angry interference. Under such circumstances human strength shrinks from the task, and nothing but a mother's love would undertake it. But notwithstanding all this, we sometimes see the success of the Christian mother, in the midst of the greatest difficulties, training up her sons and daughters in the love of truth, in the practice of goodness and religion, when the father has thrown the whole weight of his precept and example on the side of wickedness; and I have felt, at such times, that a mother's influence, if wisely and prayerfully exerted, is second only to that of God himself. Let her not despair. Still let her be hopeful against hope, and her love, through the blessing of God, will ultimately prevail.

Seldom, however, is her work so discouraging. Generally she has a better field of working, in which a moderate degree of exertion, together with a true Christian character in herself, will secure an answer to her prayers. In the majority of families, other influences are not very decided, either for good or evil, and become one or the other according to that of the mother's character. The atmosphere which her children breathe is that of religion or irreligion, of worldliness or of piety, at her bidding. They may advance in goodness almost by a natural growth, and from their early lisping of the Lord's Prayer till their characters are confirmed in goodness, her hand leads them so gently, that they do not know how much they owe to her, until they themselves have children to guide. I heard it said of one who was eminent in goodness, that it was impossible to understand how he could be so pure, so excellent, until you had seen and known his mother; but that in her face and manners you would at once read the whole history. Perhaps it was not saying too much. It is difficult to estimate how large a part of the excellence of the best men is due to a mother's counsel, and is the reflection of a mother's character. We do not need to be taught that the mother of Howard was a good woman, and the mother of Washington is revered in history almost as much as Washington himself.

On the other hand, there must be another side to the picture. The frivolous and heartless woman, who makes religion secondary to fashion, who pursues pleasure so eagerly as to forget her duty, who neglects her children and intrusts their moral guidance to servants or leaves it to chance, is unworthy of the place she holds, and if her children grow up well, it is a blessing she does not deserve. Nor is such a result at all probable. Their lives begin wrong and under wrong influence, and they grow up in that worldliness and irreligion, which scarcely seems to them wrong, because commended by their mother's example. It is a rare thing for the son of an irreligious woman to become religious. It is a rare thing for the daughter of one whose chief glory is in the ball-room, and to whom the pleasures of home seem tame unless its quiet is changed to revelry, to become any thing else than an indifferent copy of a bad original.

I know very well how commonplace are these remarks. If they were not commonplace they would not be worth making. It is their universally acknowledged truth that gives them importance. It is a demonstration of what we wish to prove, that the mother is the chief instrument, in God's hands, for the moral and religious training of the young. You will scarcely accuse me of exaggeration in saying, that, if this influence can be made right, all other influences will *come right.* If this influence is wrong, no other can counteract it. It is strictly true, that all our efforts in philanthropy aim to accomplish imperfectly what the mother alone can accomplish well.

But we pass to another relation in which woman is early placed, and the importance of which is not sufficiently regarded by those who hold it. No relationship is more pure than that between the SISTER and her brother. It confers no authority and implies no dependence, and is therefore free from the waywardness and constraint that might otherwise exist. The brother regards his sister with a feeling closely akin to the chivalric protection of woman in olden times, and she looks to him with correspondent affection and pride. Her influence on him is silent, seldom acknowledged, but very great. He forms his estimate of the whole sex by her character, and woman is to him an object of respect or of contempt, according to what he sees of his sister's mind and heart.

She cannot, therefore, be too careful in teaching him to respect as well as love her.

She cannot confer upon him a greater kindness, than by giving him an exalted idea of womanhood. She cannot inflict a greater injury, than by leading him to think that all women are trifling and heartless, indolent except in the pursuit of pleasure, and greedy of admiration, because he sees that such is the character of his own sister. I suspect that a good deal of the frivolous and contemptuous treatment which men show toward the other sex, would find its explanation in their want of respect towards those whom they have known in the home of their childhood. But on the other hand, the young man who has, in his mother and his sister, a correct ideal of what woman ought to be, learns to respect woman for some higher qualities than dress or ornament, and knows how to place a correct estimate on those whom he meets in society. He will make a wise selection of female friends, and be effectually guarded against those deceptions, those false appearances in public, under which many an unfortunate man has made engagements for life, which have proved a life-long disappointment.

We next speak of woman in the relation of friend and BETROTHED. There is no period in her life when her influence for good or evil is more marked than in her first strong friendship, and especially when she first engages the affections of a lover; and there is no other in which her influence is more frequently disregarded or heartlessly abused. The man who loves, and thinks himself loved in return, is easily led to a fulness of devotion, that puts him almost at the mercy of her to whom it is paid. She becomes his idol for the time; his happiness is in her power. He can see no faults which are not, by the magic of love, changed to beauties. His whole nature is exalted by the hope, the certainty, that the heart of one so pure and good is given to him. He hesitates to believe it, but at last rests happy in the conviction.

It is said that woman loves more strongly than man; but he loves more blindly. She loves him notwithstanding his faults; but his love prevents him from seeing that she has any. If, therefore, after he has thus bestowed his confidence and his best affections, he finds himself deceived, and that she, whom he thought so lovely, deserves neither respect nor love; or if, through her coquetry and fickleness, he is suddenly repulsed, by averted looks and the cold answer that she is sorry her feelings have been so much misunderstood, — how great will be the revulsion in his feelings, and how serious the injury done to his whole character! His friends may truly tell him that he has had a lucky escape, and he may believe them; but his affections are not the less blighted, and his confidence in woman gone. That disappointment in his first misplaced confidence will perhaps make him a worse man than he would otherwise have been, and serve as an excuse for many wrongs against the sex by which he has been injured. Such is the influence on him, — while perhaps she, who has wrought so great a fraud upon his credulity, plumes herself upon the conquest, and goes deliberately to work to make another.

The world is very one-sided in its judgments. If a man acts thus towards a woman, it is a crying sin and shame; but if the shadow falls on the other side, it is only a thing of daily occurrence, and some stale jest is made about "men's not dying for love." Perhaps not; and pride will make them cover over the mortification by mirth and festivity, but by so much the harder is the inward struggle. Men are not devoid of strong feeling, and, although they may not prate about betrayal and a broken heart, they feel no insult so deeply as that of which I now speak. Women should be more careful than they are. The love of a manly heart is not to be lightly regarded; it should never be trifled with. She who takes pains to fix it on herself, when she is unable to return it, and then makes it her amusement or scorn, deserves to be called by some worse name than coquette, if a worse name can be found. Her own sex should rebuke her, and from men she should receive that which is to her the only severe punishment,—neglect.

We next speak of the stronger and holier relation, in which woman becomes the WIFE. When that word is first spoken, her position in the world is completely changed. She has placed her happiness in the keeping of another, and the whole complexion of her life for good or evil is fixed, according to the character of him to whom she has surrendered her liberty. By human law his power is made so great, that she cannot easily escape from it even when harshly exercised, without bringing reproach upon herself and perhaps undeserved shame. Still more, her affections hold her so closely to him, that, long after he has deserved her contempt or hate, she continues to follow him with love. She may see his unworthiness, but she does not the less love him. He may be cold, severe, tyrannical, but a few words of tenderness make her forget it all, and his slightest assurances of love are readily believed. She may wait upon him in the sickness which guilt has brought, and witness his brutal sleep, and look with sorrow upon his bloated face, and yet under all she sees the form of him whom she first loved; the words of his first endearment still are ringing in her ears.

It is very wonderful that this should be so, but such is the fact. I have heard many women express the utmost astonishment at such devotion in others, and say that nothing would induce them to submit to such hardships, and that they could not love a man under such circumstances; but wherever the trial comes, the same experience is apt to be repeated. There is scarcely any limit to woman's devotedness, where she has once devotedly loved. You cannot judge her by any rule of reason, of expediency, of worldly advantage, or of commonplace affection. Men cannot understand it, and perhaps woman herself cannot; but it is as though she had given herself away, and had no power to recall the gift.

Such is the practical law of married life, to her who has once loved. It should teach her to be very careful in bestowing her love, and still more careful in giving her hand, as the crowning proof of love, in marriage. The risk which she runs is great enough, even at the best. If her husband is a man of good principle and worthy of being loved, he may still have faults of temper and peculiarities of taste, of which she can know nothing until the intimate relations of home make them known to her, and by which the trials of married life become sufficiently great. But let there be good moral and religious principle to begin with, and there is hope for the future. Without them, her influence will be comparatively slight, and will become less every day; but with them as the basis, she becomes his best teacher and surest guide.

Of this, which is her proper influence, we would say a few words. It is very great or very little, according to her manner of using it. If exerted chiefly in direct advice, fault-finding, and complaining, it will not accomplish much. If it is the influence of gentleness, of a well-governed temper, of cheerfulness and industry, she will find few men able to resist it, unless they are already placed by confirmed bad habits quite beyond her reach.

Whoever wishes to put himself in such circumstances that virtue will every day seem more lovely and vice more hateful, let him choose for his wife a virtuous, sensible, and religious woman, and having provided for her a home which she can call her own, not a boarding-house, but a home, let him supply it with the needful comforts and conveniences, and he may safely commit the guidance of his life to her. She will fill his house with an atmosphere of love and peace, in which the roughness of his temper will be smoothed, his happiness secured, and his whole character elevated. But unless she is amiable, sensible, and virtuous, he will find a different result. He must choose her, therefore, not for her stylish excellences, but for the substantial qualities of a good mind, good manners, and a good temper, exemplified in neatness, industry, and piety.

The wife's influence, so far as good, is measured by such qualities. Her precept may be very wise, her advice very sound, her complaints very just, and a wise man will never turn a deaf ear to them; but her example is far more efficacious. I am sometimes asked by the wife, "How shall I make my husband more religious?" But there is only one answer. Be truly religious yourself; let him see that your religion is making you sweet-tempered under the vexations of life and faithful under its trials, and if you have any influence over him, that is the surest way to exert it. If he is capable of being saved, you will by this means accomplish it. We believe that few women who pursue a course of this kind will fail, and all other methods of management and directing may be laid aside. The very name of management, on the part of a wife towards her husband, excites derision or disgust, and the least indication of it completely destroys her influence.

Finally, we speak of the DAUGHTER. Her influence is that of gentleness, obedience, and love. Before she is ten years old, her presence in the family, if she is well-mannered and well-taught, is like a gleam of sunshine. As she trips with a light step from room to room, a smile on each face follows her. She grows up in innocence and truth. She divides her mother's cares, although herself free from care. She is busied with household duties and makes them a pleasant recreation by the cheerfulness and good taste with which they are performed. She makes industrious use of her advantages, and thus repays those who provide them for her. She is wise enough to defer her own wishes to those of her parents, and to return their affection by that artless obedience which seems to be the natural expression of love. Such is the daughter as she ought to be. It is impossible to tell the pride which her parents feel in her. Her father's eye rests upon her with a quiet satisfaction that no worldly success can impart. She is the very joy of his heart, the sweetest pleasure of his life. He may love his sons equally well, but there is a shade of tenderness towards his daughter, by which she seems nearer to him.

Such is the daughter as she ought to be, and such the relation which should exist between her and her parents. Her influence then is very marked in the family circle. Her presence modifies the tone of conversation; her hands give the finishing touch to every thing in the household, so that an indefinable grace and tastefulness pervade all. Her absence is felt by all as an evil, and no one is aware how useful she has always been, and how much of their social happiness depended upon her, until they learn it by this means.

But if I were to speak with equal truthfulness of the daughter as she sometimes is, and of the relation which she holds in some families to the different members of the household, you would think that I was dealing in satire, or endeavoring to be severe. She contrives, not unfrequently, to become as absolutely useless as it is possible for a living person to be; a hinderance to all work, a preventive of all thought, a source of anxiety to her father and of unceasing trouble to her mother. She has hands and fingers, which the keys of the piano will testify and the glitter of rings, but they seem to have been made for nothing useful, and shrink like a sensitive plant from any thing that can be called work. She has feet and strength to use them, as the dance will testify, where from nine o'clock until daylight she undergoes an amount of physical exertion quite wonderful to behold; but there her energy is exhausted, and it is a weary task to walk a mile, or to wait on herself, or to do any thing else worth doing. She has undoubtedly the faculty of thought, but nothing in her conversation proves it. The introduction of a serious subject is a hint for her to retire, and to ask her opinion upon any question of literature or politics or social morality, is to her only a proof of your dulness. But introduce the subject of dress or ornament or the latest fashion, and the volubility of tongue will amaze, if it does not delight you. An excellent preparation this for the serious duties of life, and a happy prospect has he who takes such an one to share with him the real trials of the world! Still worse, it is sometimes quite shocking to see with what levity these young ladies, who would themselves be shocked if you call them young women, will incur expenses which their fathers are reluctant to pay, and spend their time in the most frivolous idleness, while their mothers work like servants in the kitchen and the nursery. To meet them on the street in their elegant array of silks and finery, for the display of which I cannot but think the street a most unsuitable place, or in the assembly-room, where full dress is measured by its costliness, not its quantity, you would not suspect that their fathers are vexed in mind how to pay for the extravagance. Sometimes their mothers, not to be thrown into the shade, share with them to the utmost of their folly, and mother and daughter are rivals for the same flippant, unmeaning attentions; and sometimes, which is worse for the one, but better for the other, the daughter's extravagance is atoned for by the mother's self-denial.

I do not mean to speak lightly or harshly, but I think there is need of speaking plainly. Good taste, not less than good morals and religion, require of the young lady to become useful as well as ornamental. It is surely to be much regretted that fashion and dress and admiration of silly men engross so much of her thoughts. Let her learn a greater degree of self-respect. Let the refinements and elegances of life continue; let her presence diffuse brightness and dispel gloomy thought; but there is no need of her being idle or useless. If she strives to be as beautiful and attractive as an angel, she ought to remember that an angel's best prerogative is to serve God faithfully, to be ready for every mission of kindness, to engage in every good work.

LECTURE IV.

EDUCATION.

"To know wisdom and instruction; to perceive the words of under standing. — Prov. i. 2.

My subject to-night is Female Education. We have heretofore spoken of the different relations in which woman is placed, and of the influence she unavoidably exerts. As society becomes more refined, her influence increases, and the question therefore becomes more important, How shall her education be so conducted as to make it good? In other words, How shall she be prepared for the proper performance of the real duties of life? It is the same question that we ask concerning men, and the importance of a right answer is then universally acknowledged; but female education is left very much to chance influences, and its direction intrusted to those who know little about what it ought to be. The remarks which I shall now make are not, however, intended to develop a system, but rather to direct your thoughts to the subject, as one which has been too much neglected.

The education of the young should have chiefly two objects in view: First, the development of the individual mind; and, secondly, to fit each individual for the position in life which will probably be held. These are the great objects of education, so far as this world alone is concerned. They belong to one sex as well as the other, and in the education of boys and young men, no one would think of neglecting them; but in the education of girls they are almost systematically disregarded, and from their neglect arise many of the mistakes which we have so much reason to lament.

In the first place, the girl or young lady should be educated with reference to her own absolute wants. She should be treated as a rational being, who has a mind to think with, duties to perform, and a soul to save. She should be taught from the beginning to make the best of her own faculties, and all the means of intellectual improvement which her parents are able to afford should be given to her. These will be great or little, according to her station in society and the degree of wealth. To the poor, the means of education must be limited, but the rich may make them as great as they please. Even the comparatively poor may make them much greater than they do, if brought to feel that the object is worth self-denial in its attainment.

But the limit of education should be fixed, not by some arbitrary idea of how much a woman ought to know, or how much it is safe to teach without spoiling her as a good housekeeper or a faithful drudge, — the principle on which the education or no education of the slave is conducted, — but the limits of female education should be fixed, as of the man's, by the capacity of the individual scholar and the external means within reach.

We say to the boy or to the young man,

"Make the best of yourself; there is no danger of your learning too much; read, study, think, for the sake of gaining maturity of judgment, and a well-disciplined mind. Lose no opportunity of attaining knowledge, whether it promises to be of immediate use or not. It is good for its own sake. Its acquisition will strengthen the mind, as exercise strengthens the body." We advise him to educate himself by all the means within his reach, not only nor chiefly that he may become a more successful merchant or a more eminent lawyer, but because the education is in itself good. It makes a man of him. It takes him out from the littleness of humanity, and interests him in the great things of life, virtue, truth, honor, beauty, and religion. It makes him independent, to a great degree, of external circumstances, and frees him from the necessity of riches, which common men feel, by giving him inward and inexhaustible wealth. The educated man can say, "My thoughts to me my kingdom are," and whether rich or poor, whether mechanic or merchant or professional scholar, whether he is a married or a lonely man, will prize his education as one of the best temporal gifts which Providence has bestowed.

But why is not this as true of woman as of man? If she is a rational being, why should we not treat her as such? Why should she not be made to feel from the days of girlhood, that it is her duty to make the best of herself, in the development of her whole mind, in the proper use of all her faculties? Why should she not be taught that knowledge is good, whether immediately useful or not; that the object of her studying is not merely to learn something which she can put to practical use when she becomes a wife and mother, but self-improvement for the improvement's sake? Why should she feel, as she often does, that the whole uses of education are attained, if she appears well in society and avoids those mistakes which betray ignorance? Why should manners be regarded as almost every thing, and the substance of a cultivated intellectual nature almost nothing?

I am afraid that comparatively few young ladies are accustomed to think of education in this way. They think of it as a schooling to be continued until the age of sixteen or seventeen, the object of which is to make them appear as well as others in their own circle, and therefore to give them an equal chance of success. They seldom think of it as the beginning of self-culture, the end of which is maturity of character and the full excellence of womanhood. We say to the boy, Make a man of yourself; be diligent, that when you come to manly years you may have a manly character. Why not say to the girl, Make a woman of yourself, that when you come to womanly years you may have a womanly character? But instead of it we say, Learn to be ladylike; remember that when you become a lady you will be quite ashamed to speak bad grammar or to enter a room in a stiff or awkward way. This is a much lower standard and reduces every thing to outside appearances. It makes the cultivation of the mind wait on the prettiness of the body. It makes a woman's education less important than her manners, and the dancing-master more indispensable than any other teacher. It degrades womanhood. It prevents the girl from seeing the real excellence of knowledge, the essential value of intellectual improvement. The young lady is not taught to respect herself for what she is, but for what she appears to be. She does not labor to improve herself because she has a mind that needs improvement, and faculties the exercise of which is the truest happiness, but her labor ceases when a certain degree of indispensable knowledge and outward polish is attained. The accomplishments which belong to the fingers and the feet are much more highly prized than those of the mind and character. Some show of study or some general plan of reading is kept up, for six or twelve months after leaving school, or until she stands at the marriage altar, and then, the great purposes of education having been secured, the further improvement of the mind is accounted unnecessary.

I do not mean to be guilty of sarcasm. It

is an easy kind of wit, which any body with an observing eye and a bad temper can attain. I should be sorry, therefore, if in my remarks I seem sarcastic, where I only intend to speak the truth; but it seems scarcely too much to say, and female writers themselves make the complaint more strongly than I would venture to do, that female education is often conducted, both in school and afterwards, as if the chief end of woman were to be married, and the chief object of education to secure a good establishment. Whatever will conduce to that end, by rendering her attractive, by making her the object of admiration, by enabling her to appear well in society and to take captive the hearts of men, — all of this is valued. No part of it is omitted. For its attainment no expense is spared. But the education needed to make her think, to make a woman of her, to teach her self-respect and self-reliance, is comparatively neglected.

This is the great error by which, more than by any thing else, woman is prevented from taking her right position in society, and from exerting her full influence. She is not educated for her own individual sake, but with reference to a certain effect to be produced on those around her, and a certain result to be attained. She is not taught to enjoy study; she is not supplied with those intellectual resources which would make her independent of praise or blame. Her ideas of usefulness and happiness are associated with her establishment in life as a married woman, and she does not prepare herself by self-education and self-discipline to be useful and happy, through the force of her own character and a cultivated mind, in whatever position she may be placed. I admit that "marriage is honorable," and that both man and woman should look forward to it with hope and joyful expectation. It is unquestionably needful to our highest usefulness and best happiness. Without it, our nature is but half developed, and we are in great danger of becoming selfish and narrow-minded. It is the appointment of Providence, the gift of Divine love, and if evaded or refused, no complete compensation for the loss can be found. Under ordinary circumstances, therefore, it is a serious misfortune to either sex to remain in what is called single, in opposition, I suppose, to the twofold blessedness. But surely this is not true of woman alone; it is equally true of man. If any thing, it is more true; for man's nature, being more rough and harsh, stands in greater need of the softening, purifying influences of the family circle.

How often do we see that among the gentlest and loveliest of their sex, everywhere welcome, everywhere honored, are those who have accounted the prize of matrimony not great enough for their acceptance! They are often the most important members of the family, the consolers of grief, the unwearied attendants in the chamber of sickness, the visitors of the poor, finding in the exercise of all beautiful charities and kindly affections, if not the full happiness of which they are capable, yet enough to make their lives a continual expression of gratitude to God, and themselves a blessing to all they love. We may know many such, and in the excellent disinterestedness of their lives, they are numbered among the saints of the earth. But how seldom do we find a parallel instance among those of my own sex! Notwithstanding all the flippant jests upon the subject, my observation leads me to think that a single life is much more fatal to man's happiness and usefulness than to woman's.

But how absurd it would be if, in his education, every thing were made to turn upon such considerations! The best way to educate him to become a good husband and father is to make him a good man. Give him the best education in your power with that view, and you do that which is best for him under all circumstances. So in woman's education, it should be conducted primarily with a view to make her a thoughtful, intelligent, well-educated person. However much her happiness may be increased by an establishment in life, she should have resources of mind and character, such as to secure her happiness at all events.

Secondly, female education should be conducted with reference to the duties which woman is called upon to fulfil in the different relations of life. Not, as I have already said, merely with a view to her entering on such relations, which is the education of outside show and accomplishments; but with reference to the duties which devolve upon her as a married woman, if circumstances lead her to become such. But this view of the subject compels me in part to repeat what I have already said; for how would you prepare one to become a good wife and a judicious mother, except by making her an intelligent and sensible woman? Other things being equal, the more highly educated a person is, in whatever situation placed, the greater his influence, and more worthy he will be of respect. This is true of one sex as well as of the other. The time has passed when it was taken for granted that the more contracted a woman's education, the more likely she is to become a good wife and mother. Those were the days when wife and servant meant nearly the same thing. Civilization has advanced too far, education is too generally diffused, for such ideas to prevail. It is expected, nay, required, that every woman in good society shall be well informed, well educated. Without this, her general influence in society is small, and even her moral influence in the domestic circle greatly lessened. For a certain degree of intellectual development is necessary to command respect, and she whose mind is narrowed by prejudice, or who is ignorant upon subjects of ordinary interest in science and literature, labors under great disadvantages in all the relations of life. She need not be afraid of knowing too much. The New England idea on the subject is correct, that every girl should be educated well enough to become a teacher in case of necessity; that with this view she should be taught thoroughly so far as she goes, and should go as far as time and opportunity allow. Such an education will unfit her to be the wife of a silly or ignorant man, unless to become his teacher; but fortunately it would take away the desire as well as the fitness.

When thus taught, she is prepared, if she becomes a wife, to be the head of her household; she is the companion and equal of her husband, capable of being his confidential adviser and assistant. He prizes her more highly in the performance of her domestic duties, because he respects her understanding. He is glad to receive counsel from her, because he sees that she has laid up materials for thought, and that she knows how to use them. It is a very good thing for a man to have a wife whom he can thus regard, and if I were preaching to young men, I would advise them to take no other. No one can tell how much he gains from daily intercourse with a well-educated and sensible woman, who at the same time performs her own duties well, so as to make his home pleasant, and is able to share his thoughts, to enter into his cares, to suggest good counsel, and to direct his mind not less than engage his heart. That is a helpmeet indeed; but to become such, a woman must not be afraid of knowledge nor unwilling to think.

A good education is equally important to the mother. As the minds of her children are developed, their "obstinate questionings of sense and outward things" are enough to puzzle even the wisest; but if she is able to lead them aright in their first seeking after truth and knowledge, to give them a taste for reading and direct them in their early choice of books, she will accomplish, almost without being aware of it, the most important part of their education. I have often remarked the difficulty, even in the best schools, of giving a good education to children, especially to girls, whose mother is illiterate or ignorant. You may provide for them the most accomplished teachers, who will carry them through books enough to entitle them to a degree in college, and yet the illiterate home-atmosphere, the uneducated mother-tongue, will half neutralize your efforts. Particularly is this true with regard to the little refinements of education, and the right cultivation of taste, which go so far towards characterizing the lady and the gentleman in society. What is learned from the mother is thoroughly learned, and it requires a great deal of drilling at school to undo her mistakes and remedy her false teaching. But if she is able to help the teacher, the school work will go on profitably, or, if circumstances require, may be dispensed with.

We do not say that the education of children should be intrusted to the mother as her duty, for she seldom has either time or strength for its performance; but it is certainly desirable for her to be competent to the task, as to her own education. She will then aid the teacher and supply the unavoidable deficiencies of school education, while, at the same time, she brings her children more immediately under her own influence, and teaches them to respect her more. A new relation to them is established, and her duties as a mother receive new dignity. Even the drudgeries of household care, from which but few ladies can escape, become less irksome, because of the spiritual and intellectual influence which she is consciously exerting over those whom she loves. No greater mistake can be made, than to suppose that an ignorant woman is more likely to become a good housekeeper than one who is well educated. It is like the antiquated mistake, that a man is spoilt for a merchant, if he is a scholar or a gentleman. A pedant, who knows just enough to be self-conceited, is out of place either in the counting-room or nursery; not because of too much education, but too little. A superficial mind, imperfectly instructed, is unfitted for all real duties. A sound and good education both stimulates and enables us to do the best we can, under whatever circumstances we are placed.

But when we speak of a good and sound education, what do we mean? It is not that which comes from school-books and a hired teacher alone, but includes the physical, moral, and religious training, which are the work chiefly of home influence and of individual self-discipline. Upon these points it is necessary to say something, for the worst mistakes in education proceed from their neglect.

Schools are good things and books are good things, but a healthy mind in a healthy body is far better, and the education which neglects these is likely to do as much harm as good. What we need for the real duties of life is not the knowledge of geography, arithmetic, and grammar, but manliness and womanliness of character. What we learn is chiefly valuable in teaching us to think, in developing the mind, in elevating the tastes, in maturing the judgment. We thus become men and women, and learn to put away childish things. But under the system of periodical cramming and display, adopted in many schools, particularly for girls, the mind is scarcely educated at all. The memory becomes apt and the perception quick, by which means a good recitation is produced; but the art of thinking is not taught. Girls very often leave school with a "finished education," whose education is scarcely begun. The materials of thought have been put in their minds, but not the ability to use them. They become women, but not womanly. They continue to think as the child, to speak as the child, and to understand as the child, and do not put away childish things. The idea of continued improvement, of self-culture, of an education which continues through life, does not even enter their minds. They have finished. As I once heard a child say, when passing from the first to the second part of his primer, that "he had got through prose and had begun poetry"; so the learning part of their life is over, and they now look for its enjoyment. Their school-books and almost all other books are laid upon the shelf, and the externals of life engage the undivided attention.

An education which leads to such a result is not worth the prices sometimes paid for it. It is a sham quite as much as a substance; but the fault is not chargeable upon the teacher alone, nor upon the school, although a part of it must rest there. It is still more chargeable upon the parents, and results from the want of right influences at home. If the moral and religious education is there neglected, the school will be building upon a sandy foundation, and the superstructure, however pretty to look at, will not endure the wear of actual life.

Let us consider this point still more carefully, for it is our principal subject this evening. The tendency at the present day is to overrate the education of books and to underrate the education of character. At the risk, therefore, of seeming to contradict myself, I would show that moral and religious culture is, beyond comparison, the most important. We can do without books; we cannot do without virtue and religion. The use of education is to make us wiser and better; otherwise it is an evil instead of a good. It is a sad thing to see the character neglected for the sake of learning, for knowledge then becomes an instrument of iniquity. After all, the education upon which we chiefly depend for our usefulness and happiness is not that which comes from books or schools. Men may learn to think without the printed page; they may learn to act usefully, wisely, and honorably, by the grace of God.

We have known men, for example, to whom the meagre education of a primary school was all with which they began life; being forced, at the age of ten or twelve years, to enter upon the career of active industry.

In the strength of a resolute purpose, and by virtue of what is properly called mother-wit, they have steadily advanced, not only in the accumulation of property, but in the attainment of useful knowledge. Their practical observation of men and things has served to develop their thinking faculties; good principle has saved them from the errors so often fatal to the young; industry has gradually supplied the place of early education; common sense has been matured by experience, until it has grown into that soundness of judgment which is the best practical wisdom, and the attainment of which is one of the highest objects of education itself. Thus, by the time the years of middle life have come, they have put themselves in the foremost ranks of society, in usefulness and respectability, among merchants, mechanics, or statesmen. Such is the history of some of the most useful and distinguished men in our country. Undoubtedly they always feel the inconvenience of imperfect early education; they would give one half they are worth to supply the deficiency The college student will smile at their mis takes in conversation, and they will smile with him, not because they despise knowledge, but because they are free from affectation.

But compare such persons with the student, who sits all day with his feet on the fender and his head in the clouds; or with the literary man, who reads every thing and does nothing; — and which is the better, the nobler, the more respectable? Nay, which is the better educated? Is not the self-education which has made a strong character and a manly life better than the really bad education which ends in idleness and a dream? The highest education of the intellect is worthless, unless the moral nature is developed and manliness secured.

Still more true is this of woman. However important the education of books, that of the heart and character is better, and goes far to take its place. The truly accomplished woman needs both, but very often the greater is sacrificed for the less. I do not advocate ignorance, but I have known women to whom the writing a letter is a serious undertaking, and the whole range of whose reading is the Bible, a prayer-book, or perhaps some time-hallowed book of sermons or a religious newspaper, who are yet sensible persons, capable of performing all the duties of life gracefully and well.

In former days, when the opportunities of education were less than now, such instances were not unfrequent. Shall I describe such a one to you? The dancing-school has done nothing for her, yet her step is quick and light, and near the bed of sickness her motions are so gentle, that the sufferer follows her with a smile on his face and a tear in his eye. She never knew the meaning of Psychology, but she has watched the working of her own heart, and the spirit of God has wrought with her spirit, until her theory of the soul is, that

“God worketh in her both to will and to do of his good pleasure.” She never opened a book of moral philosophy, but she knows enough to reject with scorn the learned theory of Paley, that selfishness is the root of all goodness, for her Bible tells her that self-denial is the beginning of virtue, and self-sacrifice its perfect consummation. Her acquaintance with geography and history is small; but she daily visits, in faith, the hallowed places where the Saviour trod, and every chosen passage of Scripture is familiar to her as household words. She has received no instruction from the singing-master, but a well-governed temper has taught her to modulate her voice, so that it is always musical and never too loud or too sharp. She looks with astonishment at the books which her children bring home from school, but while regretting her inability to aid them in their studies, she can teach them habits of attention and make them cheerful under their first discouragements; nor did it ever occur to them to despise their mother because ignorant of things which she never had opportunity to learn, for they love and revere her too much to think her ignorant of any thing. Thus will the pure mind give the most beautiful adorning; thus will a heaven-directed spirit refine and elevate itself, and gain many of the results of education, without employment of its ordinary means. It is, perhaps, an historical picture that I have drawn, but has it not some traits of beauty even to our eyes?

I need not say, that this is not my ideal of what woman ought to be. To make her such, you must add mental culture and the refinements of cultivated taste. Yet such an one has an innate nobleness that entitles her to respect and makes her greatly superior to many whose school education is far more complete. Compare her with those fancifully educated ladies, who dip into a hundred books without understanding any; who have a smattering of half a dozen languages, but cannot express themselves with simplicity in their own; who have a great deal of knowledge, but very few ideas; who have spent months and years in the acquisition of accomplishments, but have no industry to accomplish any thing useful; who have, in a word, enjoyed the advantages of polite education, but have never been taught that self-discipline which is the result of moral and religious training, and which is so indispensable to social and domestic life: and how immeasurably superior does the education of heart and life appear, to that which is chiefly of the intellect and manners, but which is, even in these departments, so imperfect.

Under a right system of education, there is no necessity of neglecting one part for the other. We say of the merchant or mechanic, that integrity of character, good judgment, and a practical knowledge of his business, are more important than general information. If he loses them, he loses every thing; but the latter ought not to be neglected. Make him a well-informed man, and his integrity, judgment, and practical knowledge will be worth twice as much as before. So in woman's education, the attainment of knowledge and improvement of the manners, the cultivation of taste, the accomplishments of music, drawing, and dancing, need not be neglected, and ought not to be; but they must be made secondary and subordinate to moral culture. They should become the handmaids of religion and virtue; branches grafted into the healthy tree of home education. The woman should regard them, first, as the means used for her own improvement and happiness, and secondly, as instruments in making her home pleasant and attractive, so as to fill her place in life gracefully and well. But very often the refinements of education are so managed as to unfit her for practical life. She is not only kept ignorant of all the details of household duty, by which means the beginning of her married life is often made a series of blunders, both mortifying and costly; but she wants the moral training of temper and disposition, without which it is so hard for her to learn. The result is sometimes, not only painful, but ludicrous. The husband not unfrequently discovers that he has made a fatal error, and, to use the quaint language of HENRY COLEMAN, "that, for all the purposes of domestic life, he might as well have put a skilfully painted picture in the parlor, and a statue of Venus de Medicis in the kitchen."

Let it be remarked, however, that the deficiency of which we now complain is not merely of skill in the management of household affairs; although this is to be regretted. It is want of that moral and religious education, which gives habits of industry and economy, a contented disposition, a cheerful heart and pleasant manners, a willingness to oblige, facility in thinking of the wants of others and corresponding forgetfulness of one's self, an amiable temper and devotedness of mind. Give her these, and she will soon learn her duty, whatever it may be. She will learn to conform herself to her circumstances in a palace or a single room. She will find that, however valuable the cultivation of her intellect has been, the habits of thoughtfulness in duty and of prayer compose "the one thing needful."

These things, let me again say, are not learned only or principally at school. They are not taught most effectually by the paid teacher nor by the printed book. They are the result of home education; they come from Bible instruction; they are the reception by the soul of heavenly influences, through the mother's example and advice, sustained by the father's authority.

Such views of the subject have always made me adverse to boarding-school education, and to all modes of educating girls away from their own homes. Peculiar circumstances may justify a resort to them, for there are exceptions to every general rule. The incompetency of mothers themselves sometimes requires it, in which case we have nothing to say but to express our regret. In a new country, also, we naturally wish to avail ourselves of the better institutions in older communities, and many go to great expense in so doing. But I believe the general rule remains, that no superiority of such institutions can counterbalance the loss of good home influences upon the female mind and character. Even to young men the trial is very great, and the apparent necessity of sending them to college, where all home influence is lost, is fraught with dangers which are often more than an offset to the advantages gained. But to the young lady the evil is far greater; for the most important part of her education consists in the harmonious development of those affections and sympathies which can be developed nowhere but at home, and at no period of life except in childhood and early youth. The home education must go on together with that of the school, so that while the head is learning from books, the heart may be learning from example, and the hands from practice. The character is thus formed while the mind is instructed, and in proportion as she learns more, she is prepared to be more useful and more happy, in whatever station of life God has placed her. She is thus educated for her position, not above it nor aside from it, and there is no danger of making her tastes too refined or her intellect too cultivated. The correcting influence of home is daily applied, so that whatever may be learned is incorporated with what is practised. But too often those educated away from home are trained for a mode of life quite different from that in which they must actually live. Through five or six years they have no one's comfort to think of but their own; no duties to perform except to study a certain number of hours, and to conduct themselves, in the presence of their teachers or of company, with a certain prim propriety, which is a sure indication that they are rude and hoydenish everywhere else. Even when such institutions are conducted on the best principles and with the best instructors, the loss of a mother's influence and care is very great and must be seriously felt; but as they are sometimes conducted, money-making concerns, with much show and little substance, they are nothing but ingenious contrivances to keep the scholar ignorant of every thing she ought to know, and to unfit her for every thing she ought to do. Too often, from such institutions, where young ladies have been kept year after year in luxury and indolence, at the expense, perhaps, of parents who have denied themselves common comforts for the sake of giving them the best advantages, they return to their homes vain and selfish, with their heads full of false notions and idle plans, looking upon industry as the height of vulgarity and upon indolence as a ladylike trait of character. The probability of their being happy at home, or of adding to the happiness of parents, is very small. If they are by nature very good girls, they may soon learn to repair the error and become sensible women; but commonly it is pretty safe to prophesy, that they will make some absurd settlement of themselves in life, and rue the consequences to the day of their death. For she who leaves home a girl, and returns a young lady, is almost a stranger to her own parents, and does not know how to make them, as they ought to be, her confidants. She has grown up away from them, and does not know how to trust herself to their sympathies. Her intimacies are very apt to be out of her own home, and although under her parents' roof, she virtually lives at a distance from them. She therefore enters upon the world untried, and almost unprotected. With more self-reliance than wisdom, she is exposed to frequent deception, and suffers frequent and sometimes the severest disappointment.

However much, therefore, we may value what are called the advantages of education, I think that very imperfect instruction at school, together with good home influences, is better than the best boarding-school education ever devised. Let parents have the wisdom to encourage our own schools, by paying as much for their daughters at home as it costs when sent abroad, and the motive for sending them away will soon cease. Let their children grow up under their own roofs, and when no longer children they will become intimate friends, and the necessity of parental authority will yield to the influence of filial love.

LECTURE V.

FOLLIES.

"Whose adorning, let it be that of a meek and quiet spirit, which is in the sight of God of great price." — 1 Peter iii. 3, 4.

If my remarks last Sunday evening were at all correct, the most important part of a woman's education is that which she must accomplish for herself. Not only during her school days, but after they are passed, the work of self-improvement should steadily go on. Her aim should be, not only to become ladylike and agreeable, but a thoughtful, well-informed, and useful woman. In other words, the education of her character and the just development of her mind is the object to be obtained. To this end her teachers may help her more or less, according to the manner in which she is taught to read, to study, and to think. The parents, and particularly the mother, may do still more by judicious instruction, and by the example of a Christian life. But after all, and above all, she must lay hold of the work herself. She must perceive its necessity, and resolve that nothing shall divert her mind from it. It is a slow work, requiring years for its faithful performance, and is in fact never completed while life continues. Humanly speaking, self-improvement is the great business of life, and is only another expression for making the best of all our faculties, for the glory of God and by his help. The young lady, therefore, instead of losing sight of it when she leaves her school-books, should feel that the work is just begun. As the carpenter, during his apprenticeship, has done little more than learn the use of his tools, and has his life's work of building and designing before him; so ought she to feel that her school education has only unlocked the door through which she must go in the further acquisition of knowledge, in the exercise of thought, in the discipline of her mind, in the formation of a complete womanly character.

We need not say that such views would materially change her course of life, particularly in the early years of womanhood. It would be for the most part an intellectual, and to many a moral regeneration, second in importance only to that spiritual birth by which we are born into the kingdom of God. Moreover, the first change would be conducive to the second, because the same hinderances which prevent intellectual and moral improvement also keep her from the religious life. By teaching her to think seriously, and to feel that the object of her life is not enjoyment, but improvement, you remove her from the frivolities which consume so much time to so little purpose; for you thereby not only teach her that such frivolity is foolish, but you take away her taste for it, except, perhaps, as an occasional recreation, to which the mind stoops when tired.

As such, we say nothing against it. Young persons must have their times of sport, and we are never so old as to dispense with them altogether. It would probably be better for many of us to recognize this necessity; for if the mind is kept on the continual stretch of serious duty, it will lose its healthy action. The teacher needs holiday more than the scholar. We must have our times of rest, when the armor of life is put off, and the weapons of its conflict laid aside, or our duties become too heavy a burden, and life itself comes to a premature close. Nor need we bring the hours of recreation under the too rigid scrutiny of reason. The scrutiny of *conscience* must be there and as strictly exercised as in our careful occupations. However pleasant it may be to do wrong, we have no right to do it; and sin committed in pursuit of pleasure is as great as if done for the sake of profit. But having made this reservation, the wisest of us can sometimes afford to lay aside our dignity and become children. As Æsop played at marbles, and the judgment of the world has since declared that under the circumstances he could not have done a wiser thing; so may our amusements sometimes be trifling, in themselves considered, for the same reason "that the bow needs to be completely unbent."

I have said this, not for its own sake, but as an introduction to other remarks. I do not wish to take the unphilosophical, untenable, and I think unchristian position, of condemning every thing in life, unless invested with soberness as a serious and momentous duty. There is danger of making life so serious as to become sad and gloomy. In that case, even our duties will be less heartily performed than if we permitted a little more of the pleasant sunlight on our path. But if we try to make it all sunlight, and ourselves to sport continually in its beams, like insects of the day, pleasure-seekers and frivolous in heart, it is a very different thing. That which may be excused or commended as an occasional recreation, becomes very unmanly or unwomanly, if made the object of daily pursuit.

Dissipation is a hard word, and to say that a young man is dissipated is to draw a black line through his name, erasing it from the roll of those who are accounted honorable and useful in the world; for in that application it implies self-indulgence, unsteadiness of character, intemperance, and other faults destructive of usefulness and true respectability. It is perhaps too harsh a word, therefore, for our present use; but we need some corresponding term which implies the same fault of character, although the external manifestation is different. Female dissipation is pleasure-seeking, the love of admiration, devotedness to fashion, or the like. These lead to extravagance, waste of time, frivolity of character, neglect of duty, unwomanliness of conduct; in a word, to a selfish, worldly, and irreligious life. All this may be without a single act which can be called crime, almost without any thing which, taken by itself, can be called sinful. It is the making a business of pleasure; the surrendering one's self, body and mind, to the capricious rules of fashion and to the superficial demands of social life; so that the enormous accumulation of trifles rests upon the soul with almost as heavy weight as the greater faults which men commit. A single feather may be an ornament; but you may be buried under feathers, as effectually as under the baser earth. Each day and hour may seem to be lightly, almost harmlessly spent. As you seek to defend each separate act, we may admit that there is no great harm in it; if really by itself, no harm at all. But a whole winter spent in such a way, months and years, sometimes a whole life, consecrated, nay, desecrated to amusement as the real occupation of the mind and heart, — surely we need no harsh words to make the folly and the sinfulness of such a course appear.

The young lady finishes her school days with the feeling of one who has escaped from thraldom. She has looked forward to the day with longing eyes and exaggerated expectations. Her studies have perhaps been pursued more closely, because the time when she could stop studying was so near. She has labored, as if the whole education of her mind must be compressed into a few years, at the close of which she would be done with books, except by way of amusement, for ever. The day comes at last, although deferred by parental command as long as possible, and at the age when the mind is just attaining that maturity of judgment which would make her studies of real use, she passes in a month's time from the discipline of girlhood to the recognized position of a young lady in society. She is now diligently prepared to "come out,"—as though the whole work of in-door education were complete. The parents are given to understand that no expense is to be spared, particularly for her first season, and that every thing depends upon a good impression being now made. The house is thrown open for company, and the game of life fairly begun. Cards and invitations pour in and afford the principal reading, and dress is the all-absorbing subject of thought. Day after day is given to visits of etiquette, to evening receptions, to prolonged consultations about the latest fashion, and to other things which are as nearly nothing as it is in the nature of any thing to be. The night is not spared, but at nine or ten o'clock — a young person's proper time for retiring to rest — the elaborate and long-studied arrangement of dress is complete, and the feverish excitement of the ball-room begun, to be continued with increasing hilarity until the night yields to morning. She returns home too excited to feel weary, but compelled to find, in the early part of the next day, the repose needed for a renewal of the like occupations, which soon grow to — what shall I call it but dissipation? In this way weeks and months pass in alternating languor and excitement; in the intense pursuit of pleasure, which is more than half the time falsely so called.

Now the first and most obvious fault to be found with such modes of life is in the lamentable and destructive waste of time. If all this fashionable dissipation were in itself unobjectionable, which is far from the truth, yet is it not a sad thing for a woman to give so much of the best part of her life to trivial amusement? It cannot be called recreation, for it is itself a business which engrosses the thoughts, occupies nearly all the time, and leaves neither strength nor inclination for any thing else. The young lady under such circumstances may at first have some vague purpose of self-improvement and some general plan of reading, but she will soon find it impracticable, and after a few well-intended but spasmodic efforts, will defer its execution to the close of the season, when she expects to have more time and less interruption. But unfortunately, when the time comes, the inclination is very likely to be gone. Three or four months spent in a continued round of company are a bad preparation for the quiet hours of reading and reflection. The excitement of the mind subsides, as the outward stimulants are withdrawn, and a corresponding lassitude is the inevitable result. The body itself needs rest, and generally speaking, in the fashionable world, several weeks or months, and sometimes the whole summer, must be devoted to recuperate the energies and renew the flow of animal spirits, in preparation for another season, in which the same follies will be repeated.

How undignified, may I not say how unchristian, is such a life! How completely it must unfit those who follow it for the duties and the enjoyment of home! What room does it leave for intellectual self-culture, or religious self-discipline? Who can wonder that the young, who pass directly from their school days to such a career as this, never attain maturity of character, but continue, even after they have become wives and mothers, to devote themselves to the pursuit of pleasure, the willing devotees of fashion? What wonder is it that female education is at so low a mark, and woman's influence so small compared with what it should be when so many are thus neglectful of their own improvement and eager in the pursuit of trifles!

A second objection to the mode of life now described is in the extravagance to which it leads. This is a great and increasing evil among us. There scarcely seems to be any limit to the cost of living required by fashionable life. Each one tries to outdo the other, until a style of dress and entertainment is established, enough to impoverish all but the very rich, and to exclude all prudent and sensible persons from the competition. But unfortunately few of us are either prudent or sensible in such things. As our children grow up, we do not wish to seclude them from the world, and our own social ambition excites us to do as others do. How far the fault is chargeable to the mother and daughter, and how far to the husband and father, we shall not seek to determine; but it belongs to my present subject to say, that the extravagance into which the young lady is led by fashionable life, and in which she is encouraged too often by the precepts and example of her mother, is frequently beyond the bounds both of reason and good taste. Even where there is great wealth, it is barely excusable, for the greatest wealth does not justify wastefulness. But when, as the case commonly is, the expenditure is not measured by the income, the evil and the sin are both increased. I do not ask for sumptuary laws, to bring our mode of living under strict and arbitrary rules; nor do

I wish that the elegances of dress and entertainment should be altogether abated. But I do wish that a higher standard of taste could prevail, and that extravagance for extravagance' sake were accounted vulgar. The lady who loads herself with jewelry and the annual cost of whose wardrobe would support an orphan asylum, seems to me to have departed as far from the canons of correct taste as from those of propriety. Her apparel ceases to increase her beauty, when admired only for its splendor, and ornament fails in its purpose when it diverts attention from the wearer. The lady forgets herself, I think, and compromises her dignity, when she becomes, as it were, an advertisement for the jeweller and milliner.

I know how absolute are the requirements of fashion, nor would I be so foolish as to put myself in direct opposition thereto. We may read in HUME'S History, that for two centuries the whole priesthood of England expended their strength against certain insignificant fashions; but the historian says, that although they were able to excite the whole community to the wars of the Crusades, in which both blood and treasure were poured out like water, the pointed shoes, with chains appended to the knee, continued in spite of them.

We are compelled, almost, to conform ourselves, in some measure, to the usages of the world. Sound morality does not require, and good taste does not permit us to become the object of remark in our manner of dress and living. Up to a certain point it is a matter of indifference, in which a sensible person will be content to follow those who wish to lead, and the best general rule in all such things is to avoid making one's self conspicuous. The moment that we violate this rule, we offend against good taste, whether it be by the affected disregard of custom, or by going to the extreme of fashion and display. When the dress is so splendid, that one can hardly help thinking that she who wears it came only to be looked at, she is giving evidence neither of sound judgment nor good taste. It should be painful to her, I think, to know that all eyes are turned towards her, and the admiring gaze mingled with astonishment. But the love of admiration is very greedy and not very discriminating. The young gentleman appropriates to himself the praise which belongs to his tailor or to his horse, with as much self-complacency as if properly his own; and the young lady is almost as proud of the compliments lavished upon her adorning, as if they were paid to her own beauty or intellectual accomplishments. Nor is it only the admiration of the judicious that gives pleasure. The praise, bought at the expense of so much money and time, is chiefly that of thoughtless, shallow-minded people, of either sex, who are half the time insincere in their commendations, and who indemnify themselves for the flattery given to one, by ridicule cast upon another,— both flattery and ridicule being directed to the same subject, present or absent.

There is no passion which needs more careful watching than this of which we now speak, the love of praise. Under the best circumstances, when excited by real qualities of mind and character, and when the praise is given by those whose good opinion is worth having, it is dangerous. It spoils the simplicity of our characters, and takes the place of higher motives of conduct. But they who pride themselves on the admiration of silly persons, paid to outside accomplishments, are in a fair way to become silly themselves.

Another material objection to the dissipations of fashionable life is found in the frequent sacrifice of health. The physical education of women is, at the best, too much disregarded in this country. From the early life of the school-girl there is a systematic neglect of exercise, which prevents her from gaining bodily strength. She is kept at her desk as many hours as the boy, but carefully discouraged from entering into out-of-door games like those which give to his blood renewed and healthy circulation. Primness of demeanor and what is called ladylike conduct are enforced upon her, at eight years old, when it would be much more natural to enjoy herself as a child. Her dress, also, is arranged with regard to looks rather than comfort, and she does not learn to bear the exposure of a changing climate. There is, therefore, great need of reform. Every school should have its exercise-room and its play-ground, where good, honest, and hearty exercise can be taken. Let the chest be developed, and the arms become strong. The symmetry of the most graceful figure will not be impaired by healthy development of the muscles, while the prospect of a useful and happy life is greatly increased.

But we cannot pursue the subject now. It is enough to refer to what every body knows, that the majority of girls now leave school with very imperfect health. Two thirds of the time, some bad tendency in the constitution has been confirmed, and distressing headaches, or weakness of the spine, or susceptibility to pulmonary disorders, is the result. It is quite a luxury to see a young lady of sixteen in the enjoyment of sincere and vigorous health, with a fresh natural color and a well-developed form.

This is not a promising state of things for

their entrance on life; but if, for two or three years afterward, they could live a rational life, engaged in household duties, or in healthful walking and riding, and in the enjoyment of social amusements without dissipation or unreasonable exposure, the injuries of the school life would probably be, to a great extent, repaired. The body would regain its vigor, and a good measure of womanly health be secured. At present, no such opportunity is allowed. Before the school days are finished, the social dissipation begins. The lessons are learned with double diligence, so that the evening and night may be given to the ball-room. Through the next day compliments and philosophy struggle for the mastery, and the whole emulation of the school is required to keep the overtasked body from yielding to fatigue.

The appetite is thus whetted for the pleasures of society, and as soon as the last school examination has been endured, they are entered upon with the eagerness of fresh delight. She who is not strong enough to walk a few squares on a cold day or in the muddy street, is quite able to spend half the day with the dress-maker, and all night in the dance. Whatever degree of exposure fashion may require, she submits to with alacrity, and does not learn until months or years are past, how fatal is the result to her physical health. Even after health is already gone, the love of excitement remains; and I have known some to rise from a sick-bed, throwing off the covering of blankets for a covering of gauze, and mistaking the feverishness of pulse for the natural return of strength. How frequently, when the winter is over, and the days of Lent or the close of the season require the resumption of a more staid manner of life, do we see young ladies pale and languid, almost as if recovering from a long sickness! How can we then wonder that the number of healthy women, in the higher classes of society, is so small? The causes which I have now named explain it at least in part, and while the laws of the physical nature are so much neglected at school, and so much outraged in the earlier years of womanhood, there seems to be no reasonable hope of amendment. It is said by the defenders of such customs, that the exercise of dancing is so healthful as to compensate for the exposure. But exercise in a heated and overcrowded room is not of much value, although I admit that the dance, when conducted in such a manner as not to offend against modesty, is the least objectionable feature of the ball-room or fashionable party. The chief objections are found in late hours, prolonged excitement, insufficient apparel, extravagance, and foolish indulgence at the supper-table. If these could be removed or moderated, if they could be brought within the bounds of reason, if they were so arranged that a sensible man or woman could approve of them, while engaging in them, we should have less fault to find. What prospect there may be of such a result, I do not know. From one step to another, we are learning to imitate the most foolish customs of European society, and in many respects succeed in going beyond our teachers. The best hope is, that the extreme point may be soon reached, and then, as some further change will be indispensable, for the sake of novelty, if nothing else, good sense may become fashionable.

I am fully aware of the degree to which I am laying myself open to censure. The charge of impertinence or of ministerial meddling would not in the least surprise me. It may be said that I am talking of things I know nothing about. It may be accounted absurd for one who lives in almost complete seclusion from society, to indulge in strictures upon it. But perhaps he who stands upon the outside may become, for that reason, a more competent observer. In the review of an army, one does not mingle in the ranks, except for occasional inspection, but stands at such a distance as to see the combined movement. You must not be too near an edifice, if you would perceive its true proportions. With regard to social customs, it requires only a common faculty of observation to know what the world is; and to one who is accustomed to judge of human nature, slight indications are enough to lead to a correct result. Besides, I do not speak as a cynical philosopher, who would put sour into every sweet, and frown upon enjoyment merely because it is enjoyed. I am not a preacher of gloom or of puritanism, but of moderation. That is all I would ask, if I had the power to command. It seems to me that the young, and sometimes those who are not young, are too thoughtless in the pursuit of pleasure. Social enjoyment degenerates into dissipation, intellectual improvement is effectually stopped, and deterioration of character effectually begun. Harmless things become sinful by excess, and if in themselves not harmless, but pernicious, they become an increasing and at last a fatal evil.

At least, no one will deny that the longer such a course of life is continued, and the more heartily pursued, the less prepared one must be for the real duties of woman's life. She who lives on the daily food of admiration, whose happiness depends more and more upon the excitement of company, who gives the greater part of her time to trifles light as air, and expends money as though it cost no labor to earn it, is in a very bad progress of self-education. The quiet of home gradually becomes distasteful, the mind is almost incapacitated for serious thought, habits of extravagance are confirmed, and false notions of gentility introduced; altogether affording not very good promise of a life of industry, economy, self-denial, and other homely virtues, without which home itself becomes miserable. A single season of such preparation is a permanent injury to the character; a succession of them for several years is enough to ruin almost any. A great deal of the unhappiness of married life is to be ascribed to this cause; for the wife must either make a complete change from the previous mode of living and in the sources of her enjoyment, a change which, if not compulsory, requires more strength of character than the majority possess; or she must continue in the same habits of pleasure-seeking, thereby neglecting her most important duties, and exerting a bad influence over those she loves. Her husband finds that the expense of married life is far greater than he anticipated, and the comfort less. He will perhaps make the attempt to gain the domestic bliss of which he has read in books; but if his wife has no relish for reading, and accounts a quiet and a dull evening one and the same thing, he will probably soon yield the point, if not to her persuasions, yet to his own desire to please her. He will, perhaps, remain at board as long as he can, to avoid the more expensive parts of fashionable life, or enable himself to meet them, but will soon fall upon a scale of expenditure which it demands his utmost exertions to meet. So far as that goes, great success in business and untiring industry may make it right, and if he obtained his money's worth, it would be a small matter. But as the social comfort is very apt to become less as the expenditure increases; as he must see that his hard working on one side is only to supply means of wastefulness on the other, and that his children are growing up with notions of life which nothing but continued riches can satisfy; we need not wonder that fault-finding and discontent sometimes prevail. How much better it would be, if young persons of both sexes could form habits of more quiet enjoyment, and learn to entertain more moderate expectations. If their minds were sufficiently educated to enjoy reading and rational conversation; if the cheerful industry of the domestic circle had a charm in their eyes beyond that of the theatre or ball-room; if they knew the value of money when expended for the poor and suffering, or for the purchase of solid comforts for themselves and others, — how great would be the gain to the young themselves and to society at large! how much better would the promise of life become to those who trust their happiness to each others' keeping, in the holy bonds of matrimony!

Let the blame, as it now stands, be equally divided, if you please; but my present subject leads me to say, that if the fault could be corrected on woman's side, her influence would soon correct it on the other. If the young wife is prepared by the graces of her character, as well as of her person, to make the quiet hours pass pleasantly, if her tastes lead her to find her own happiness at home, her husband will soon learn that his happiness is also there. The pleasures of the world would be rarely sought, because they would not be enjoyed. Life would become more rational, not less cheerful. It would take a higher tone, with which the dissipation of fashionable life would produce an unpleasant discord, — to be introduced perhaps occasionally as a discord into music, that it may be speedily resolved by a return to the social harmony. Who will deny that it would be a change for the better? But the only thing needed to effect it is a change of taste, of character, in those whom the change would benefit.

May I, therefore, in bringing my present discourse toward a conclusion, make some suggestions to those whom I now chiefly address, not so much with the view of giving instruction as of exciting thought. For this is the great trouble. There is no danger of their coming to a wrong decision, if they can only be aroused to the necessity of thinking for themselves, and of acting under a sense of their individual responsibility to God.

I would urge them, therefore, in the first place, to have some general plan of life. Let there be a fixed purpose of intellectual and moral improvement. Do not let one week after another pass, until the whole year is gone, under influences of which you scarcely know whether they are good or bad. Let a part of each day be given to reading, and let a part of the reading be diligent study. Take pains to form habits of industry, and do not be afraid of bodily exercise. Remember that time is a precious gift, for which you are responsible to God. If wasted, your mind, your soul, is wasted with it.

Be not blind followers of fashion. To some extent you must undoubtedly yield to its imperious demands; but conscience has its demands also. There is a right and wrong in fashion, as in every thing else. The most delicate sense of modesty should not be violated, if all the fashionists of Paris and all the dancing-masters of Europe were to demand it. Poetry tells us that "the chariest maid is prodigal enough, if she unveil her beauties to the moon," and the older she grows, — particularly if the maiden becomes a wife, — the less of poetry and the more of truth do the lines contain. Simplicity of taste is generally good taste, and extravagance always tends to vulgarity. Eagerness for display shows want of self-respect. With regard to apparel, therefore, it is a good rule, that, as to costliness, too little is better than too much; and as to quantity, too much is better than too little.

Be not devotees of pleasure. There is no harm in mirth or in laughter, and where there is a healthy flow of spirits, they must have vent; but they do not the less need wholesome restraint and judicious direction. The exercise of a discriminating conscience is nowhere needed more than in the choice of our amusements, and in determining their limits.

Every woman and every man should make it a question, not only of pleasantness and custom, but of right and wrong, what amusements are to be selected, and how far and in what way to be followed. I speak somewhat ignorantly here, but I suppose that every young lady, upon her first entering society, sees many things to shock her sense of propriety, but to which she gradually becomes accustomed and which she soon learns to adopt. It would be better if the tenderness of conscience could be kept, even at the risk of seeming demure.

If we could remove from popular amusements and from fashionable modes of entertainment, every thing objectionable, greater moderation would probably be exercised in their pursuit. I am told by those who seem to know, that few persons become very fond of cards, or other games of chance, unless the excitement of loss and gain is added; not so much because they care for the money, as for the excitement itself. And so with many other things, a certain degree of impropriety, a dash of wrong, seems to add zest to the amusement. The questionable character of a dance seems to give it a preference over other modes of the same amusement which are certainly harmless. The masquerade, which, even if it were harmless at first, is acknowledged to be peculiarly open to abuse, and in itself one of the most dangerous amusements in a community so mixed and excitable as ours, almost immediately becomes fashionable, although, I hope, not permanently so. The wrong allusions to which the drama frequently descends, and stage exhibitions, the propriety of which is more than doubtful, are often greeted with most hearty applause. It is not, I suppose, that in these things there is a deliberate seeking for wrong, but, like the bread eaten in secret, the hesitation which conscience excites and the flutter of the feelings produce an excitement of the whole nature, and give one something like the feeling of daring and victory, together with the laughter and the mirth. The longing after forbidden things is not confined to children, and what a scrupulous conscience forbids, if not with a stern but a questioning voice, is sometimes all the more freshly enjoyed. It is an element in human nature, until purified by religion, of which we have no reason to be proud, and it should make us very careful in the choice of our pleasures. For as the palate becomes used to stimulants and spices, and continually requires a stronger infusion, so will one pleasure after another seem tame and a higher relish be required. We need, therefore, a great deal of self-watchfulness. I know too little of such subjects to enter into detail, but it is safe to take this general rule, that, in all questionable cases, it is better to give the benefit of the doubt to modesty and a tender conscience.

Finally: the givers of advice are proverbially loquacious, and I will conclude abruptly, although not easier to do so than it would have been a half-hour ago. The correctness of my remarks may be called into question; but this would not disturb me. I desire, as I have repeatedly said, not so much to direct your thoughts, as to excite them. Where there is a general good intention, as I presume there is with all who hear me, to think at all upon such subjects is to think correctly. A great deal of what has been said is applicable to one sex as well as the other, and a part of the time I have been preaching to myself, not less than to you. We should all be seekers together for that wisdom "which guides the young, with innocence, in pleasure's path to tread"; we should remember that life is a reality, upon which eternal realities depend. The best adorning, therefore, even to the young and beautiful, is not that of worldly elegance, "but a meek and quiet spirit, which is in the sight of God of great price."

LECTURE VI.

WOMAN'S MISSION.

"Let your light so shine before men, that they may see your good works, and glorify your Father which is in heaven." — Matthew v. 16.

My object this evening will be to show the relation which woman holds to morality and religion. I shall attempt to prove that she is bound, not only by a general sense of duty, but by peculiar obligations, to promote those great interests, both directly and indirectly, by every means in her power.

It needs but little consideration to see that her own interests, individually and as a sex, are in fact inseparable from those of which I speak. Whenever she speaks a word against them, whenever she does any thing, either deliberately or carelessly, to their prejudice, she becomes her own worst enemy. Similar remarks may indeed apply to man; for we all gain in comfort and happiness by the advancement of the highest interests of society; but although true of all, it is particularly true of woman.

Her whole dignity, even her respectability, depends upon the degree of her virtue. She is made the equal and helpmeet of man much more by her moral qualities than by those which are purely intellectual. Her mind, purified by communion with Heaven, elevated by strong and self-denying affections, rises to an equality, often to more than equality, with that of the profoundest scholar or the wisest philosopher. But her road to this eminence is seldom through the regions of abstract thought or abstruse inquiry, which she seldom enjoys and for which the ordinary occupations of her life afford but little opportunity. To a few women, now and then, at long intervals in the world's history, the opportunity and ability are given of rising to fame and honor independently of those qualities which adorn her moral character; but such instances are rare, and when they occur, fail to excite admiration. Generally speaking, they are lowered in our respect by the apparent exaltation.

Men may command a certain degree of respect, and may rise to a great height of worldly dignity, although depraved in character. I am speaking now of the world as it is, not as it ought to be; and the history of our own land, as well as every other, proves what I say. A man may command admiration as a scholar or as a statesman, as historian, poet, or novelist; his fame may be so extended that his writings are found on every table, and his name on every tongue, although he himself may be notoriously a bad man and his works confessedly impure.

We might give many instances, if needful, in proof of this assertion; but your own memory will supply them. We do not say that one can rise to the highest eminence under such conditions, or that his fame will be of the most enduring kind; for I believe that, almost without exception, the SHAKSPEARES and MILTONS and NEWTONS are men who in their lives have been pure, and in their writings advocates of goodness. But still, there are the BYRONS and VOLTAIRES and a hundred others, more than enough to prove my assertion. Distinguished men are tried, at the bar of public opinion, too much by the laws of intellect, and too little by those of morality. But to women a stricter rule is applied. What would become of the fame of Miss EDGEWORTH, Mrs. OPIE, or HANNAH MORE, if you divest their works of a pure moral tone, or their characters of good moral principles? Can you imagine a female author to occupy a position like that of STERNE, or SWIFT, or even like that of HUME, or GIBBON? What influence would they have, and what degree of respect would they command? Let the names of FRANCES WRIGHT, recently dead, or of Madame GEORGE SAND, still living, a byword and an astonishment, give a sufficient answer. The pages of biography give no instance of more complete or sad disappointment in life, than that experienced by her whom I have just named as having recently died. I remember her distinctly when she first came to this country, the daughter of a noble family in Scotland, and received with cordial hospitality at the seat of government, by those whose friendship conferred distinction. I remember her tall and commanding presence and her keen intellectual glance, not quite womanly, perhaps, but full of vigor, and awakening thought in those to whom it was directed. She came in company with the great LA FAYETTE, and for a time divided with him the public attention. She gave promise of rising to the highest fame, and our country began to congratulate itself at her coming. But her mind was already divorced from religious faith; she hoped to be wiser than the Gospel, and to reorganize society under laws of less restraint; and although her general purpose seems to have been good, her whole life became a mistake, a sadness, and a loss. She accomplished nothing that she had hoped to accomplish; her fame passed into unenviable notoriety; she became a warning, instead of an example, to her sex, and at last, although possessed of great property by inheritance, she died among strangers, with no kindred hand to close her eyes, and the place which once knew her shall know her no more for ever. So strict is the standard by which woman's fame is measured. The first requisition is that she shall stand upon the side of virtue and religion, or her fame becomes infamy, and her name a reproach. No degree of talent will save her from it, and even her mistakes, though well intended, if they place her in opposition to the great interests of society, are visited upon her as crimes.

In the more private circles of life, also, moral delinquency is punished with greater sternness in woman than in man. This proceeds, in part, from the fact, that men make the laws and fix public opinion, and are therefore more lenient to their own sins; perhaps because they better understand their own temptations, and perhaps because it is always easier to see the mote in another's eye, than the beam in one's own. It is a difference, therefore, caused partly by selfishness, and is in so far unjust.

We have a right to complain and we do complain of the injustice, when woman is trampled under foot and shut out from all possible return to a good life, and almost from the hope of salvation, for the same sins that are easily excused in man. But we believe that the apparent injustice proceeds also in part from the difference in the natural elements of the male and female character, and sometimes the greater severity of which we speak is indicative of greater respect for woman's moral nature, and not of unjust feelings.

A good woman is the equal of a good man. I do not mean by offsetting the higher moral qualities of the one against the higher intellectual qualities of the other; but her pure and moral nature, when rightly cultivated, elevates and ennobles the intellectual, and gives her a clearness of thought, an accuracy of judgment, and a comprehensiveness of understanding, which place her fairly upon a level with the highest. We need not, therefore, be surprised at the saying of an eminent statesman, that he had never taken a wrong course in public affairs, when he had first asked his wife's opinion concerning it. He found her conclusion generally correct, even when she could not tell the exact premises from which derived. Perhaps many of us who are not statesmen would gain by similar consultation with those whom we now scarcely condescend to inform whether we are rich or poor, and whom we seldom allow to share our more serious thoughts. There would be a great many less failures in business, and a great deal less wildness of speculation, if all to whom Providence has given good wives could also obtain wisdom enough to advise with them in the conduct of their affairs. For a sensible woman will generally advise moderation, and will readily consent to a diminution of luxury or comfort, rather than have her husband a slave to business, or engaged in pursuits which his judgment declares unsafe, or his conscience wrong. The wife is very often guilty of great extravagance, because ignorant of the cost at which it is maintained. She does not know the wear and tear of mind and conscience to which the splendor of the household often subjects those who support it. It would, therefore, be a great gain to both parties, if she were more fully informed, where she is so deeply interested. Let the husband treat her as his equal and he will find that she is fully so.

But, on the other hand, an indifferent or bad woman does not rise to the poor equality with an indifferent or bad man. Little as may be our respect for a man without good principles, a woman without good principles deserves and will receive less. We do not mean that her sin before God is greater, but that her present degradation is more deep. The sin of every departure from right is immutably the same, whether by man or woman, by the monarch or the beggar, by the scholar or the clown; or we should rather say, it is varied in degree only by the strength of temptation, the power of resistance, and other circumstances of which God alone can judge correctly; and under this judgment, woman may deserve the lighter sentence as often as man. But man is composed of harsher material, and the stain left by sin, though equally deep, is not equally evident. As a statue made of granite or freestone seems uninjured by the handling, when the marble is soiled by the dust falling on it, and stained by the lightest touch, so with the nature of woman; her organization is the more delicate, and by so much the more her worth depends upon keeping that delicacy unimpaired. She lives more in her affections, and by so much the more they must be kept pure and generous, to secure either her happiness or the beauty of her charactcr. By goodness and truth, by modesty and a gentle·demeanor, she becomes, in the performance of her humblest duties, an object of admiration; in the lowliest sphere worthy of the highest honor. But sin destroys her utterly. It seems to leave nothing in her to love or respect. Every wrong thought, every deviation from modesty, every unladylike or unwomanly action, every selfish or worldly pursuit, degrades her in mind, in heart, in character. No strength of intellect, no mental accomplishments, no scholar-like attainments, much less can beauty and elegance and a fashionable manner, compensate for the loss. Woman's only strength is in her moral excellence. She cannot find her true dignity apart from goodness. That is the only means by which she can obtain the respect and consideration on which her happiness depends.

Again, she has a great deal at stake in the moral and religious character of the community where she lives. The regard paid to woman in society depends very much upon the standard of public morality. If she wishes to be more highly respected, and her claims to be more justly considered, her best means of accomplishing it is to labor for the general diffusion of knowledge, refinement, and virtue. So true is this, that you may measure the moral elevation of a community by the estimation in which woman is held. As we look over the different nations of the earth, we cannot find a single exception to this rule.

Learn the manner in which woman is regarded, and you can tell the standard of morality, of refinement, of general intelligence. Of course we do not now refer to her treatment in courts and palaces, but to the place she is allowed to hold in social life generally. Nor do we mean by respectful treatment the deferential bowing and complimentary salutations, in which the most heartless profligates are sometimes most profuse; but we mean the genuine respect which leads to justice and generosity in our treatment of woman, to giving her the protection which is her due, to providing for her proper means of education, to placing her in all things in the honorable position to which she has a rightful claim. In proportion as we become civilized, in proportion as man rises to the knowledge of his spiritual wants and interests, in proportion as he becomes wise and good, this treatment is extended to her. The Christian religion proves itself to be that of the highest civilization by this as much as by any thing else, the position in social life which it awards to her. Therefore, if she would be a friend of her own sex, if she understands her own highest interests, it should be her prime object to exert all her influence in the promotion of truth and righteousness.

Again, we are led to the same result, because the consequences of all wicked customs in society affect women more nearly than men. Even where man is the greater sinner, woman is the greater sufferer. She is physically the weaker, and the strength of man, if unrestrained by principle, compels her to submit to insult and suffering. She is confined to the narrow limits of home, and is there subject to petulance, anger, and unreasonable demands, and even to vile treatment, from men who are stupid enough to feel themselves, and sometimes brutish enough to call themselves, her masters. In a community where licentiousness prevails, where dissipation is fashionable, and the dramshop a place of daily resort, you may see disorder and contention in the streets, and evidences enough of the prevailing corruption may meet your eye and ear: but if you would know the worst, follow the drunkard to his home; see his children shrink away from his approach; see his wife weeping for herself and for them, but thoughtful of him, receiving him with kindness, but repaid with a curse or a blow, — bound to him even in his degraded state, by an amazing fondness, which makes her at once his victim and his slave. If the wife is unreasonable and wicked, the husband may escape from her, and in active pursuits of industry or the gay companionship of the world find partial relief. But for her there is no retreat, no escape, nay, the very nobleness of her nature and the disinterestedness of her affections sometimes prevent her from accepting deliverance, if offered; and through the long, dreary day, with persevering care and decreasing means, she is compelled to labor in sorrow of heart, in mortification of soul, until the closing hours bring back the suffering.

It is one of the great mysteries of Providence that the sins of the guilty are visited on the innocent; and therefore, if woman would be happy, it is not enough to be pure and good herself, she must strive to promote purity and goodness among those with whom her lot is cast, and in society at large. She can escape from servitude and suffering only when men become worthy of loving her, and herself worthy of being loved.

The social interests of women are therefore inseparable from those of good order and social morality; still more are they inseparable from religion. I believe that, if she understands her own nature or her own interests, she will be religious herself and do all she can to promote religion.

In the first place, she is herself led to a religious life by the natural tendency of her affections. Her nature disposes her to trust, to confide, to believe, to hope. Doubt and distrust are painful to her, and she is happier to believe without evidence than not to believe at all. The strength of her affections and the irrepressible yearning of her heart for those that are dead; the consciousness of inexhaustible fountains of love in her soul, which time has only opened, when death comes to close them; the tenderness of her conscience, and, in short, the whole construction of her mind and heart, make it pleasant for her to receive the doctrines of life and immortality brought to light. She more easily perceives the obligation and the glory of self-sacrifice. She trusts in God because she loves to trust. She worships him because she loves to revere. When she explores the unknown depths of her heart, unknown even to herself, she cannot believe that those whom she loves so much shall perish for ever because their frail bodies die, and although her mind may listen to the whispering voice of doubt, her heart is strong enough to silence or to overrule it.

Sceptical men sometimes scoff at religion, by saying that the majority of believers are women; but they prove, thereby, the folly of their own hearts, rather than the depth of their understanding. The tendency of woman's nature to religion is her best praise. It is not because she is unable to think, but because she is compelled to feel. Her mind is capable of discerning the verbal objections and the more serious difficulties, on account of which religion is rejected by so many; but they all sink into insignificance, compared with the infinite consolation which religion gives; they all fade away under the necessity, which her heart creates, of a God in whom she can trust, of a Redeemer in whom she can hope, of a heaven where her loved ones dwell.

Religious scepticism is not the proof of a strong mind. Recall the names of the greatest and wisest men that ever lived, and almost without exception their authority is on the side of religion. Confucius and Zoroaster, Homer and Socrates and Plato, Virgil and Cicero and Tacitus, together with nearly all of whom ancient history speaks as the heroes of the race, the benefactors of mankind, were confirmed believers in religious truth, according to the best light that God gave to them. There is scarcely an exception, among all whose names history has thought worth preserving. In more modern times, how many of the most acute metaphysicians, the most enlightened statesmen, the most thorough scholars, may be named as defenders of the Christian faith! In our own country the testimony of the wise and good in favor of religion is peculiarly strong. Nearly all of our statesmen, nearly all of our best writers and of our first poets and philanthropists, have been men of religion; while among those who have devoted themselves exclusively to religious things, as the study of their lives, are numbered not a few of the best minds the world has ever produced. The corrupt age of Charles the Second and the troubled times of the French Revolution produced sceptics by the hundred, and they flattered themselves, no doubt, that a death-blow had been given to the religion of Christ; but the result has falsified their predictions, and although the world listened to their arguments and was for a time shaken in belief, the tendency of strong minds has been a return to religion, and "wisdom is justified of her children." Take the world's history through, and scepticism shows but a poor array of strength. If we can learn any thing from observation, or if the philosophy of the mind proves any thing, then may we confidently say, that infidelity is the proof either of a bad heart or a badly balanced intellect. The strong mind yearns after eternal truth. The noble heart is not satisfied with things that perish.

The tendency of woman's nature to religion is therefore a witness in her own favor, and not against that in which she believes. Those same scoffing men of the world, who pride themselves on doubt, as if it were the profoundest, instead of a superficial exercise of the mind, are ready enough, when trouble and bereavement and sickness and death come near them, to seek shelter under the religion which was before an object of scorn; thereby proving that they were kept from being religious, not by their vigor of intellect, but by the strength of their passions. They show the superiority of their nature, by waiting until the storm drives them, with torn sails and a shattered vessel, to the safe harborage of Faith, instead of anticipating the tempest and saving themselves from loss.

Again, as it is always true that our best interests are secured by following our best impulses, so is it with woman, when she becomes the advocate of religion. The moral qualities for which she is chiefly honored receive their highest value, not from worldly considerations, but from their relation to eternity. It is because we hope to live hereafter, that purity and gentleness and love are highly esteemed. The character which is made strong by the affections is prized, because the affections will find their best development in the world to come. The majority of men pride themselves on their superior strength and their better adaptation to the rough uses of this world; but the more intelligent overlook such considerations, because the entrance on a future life will equalize them all, and the soul, whether of man or woman, which is purest in its life and noblest in its faith, will stand nearest to God. Hence it is, that religious men are always the most forward to admit the claims and maintain the rights of woman. In a community of sceptics and infidels, she is sure to be treated either as a plaything for man's amusement, or a servant for his convenience. Men have the power in their own hands and must always have it, and, unless they are restrained in its exertion by religious sympathy, and directed by religious principle, they are sure to abuse it in their treatment of the weaker sex. This is true of individuals, and still more true of communities.

When, therefore, I meet a sceptical woman, or hear her express opinions derogatory to religion, I feel like saying to her, either your mind is most unfortunately constituted, or you do not know on what your happiness depends. If she is so foolish as to affect a masculine style of thought, thinking to evince by scepticism superiority to her sex, she is giving sufficient evidence of a weak mind and narrow heart. An unbelieving woman is an anomaly, a contradiction in terms, and, although her character may be masculine, you will rarely find her intellect strong.

In Christian lands gratitude alone should bind her to religion as her best protection and defence. The Mohammedan prizes his horse higher than his wife, and the prophet himself could find no place in heaven for her whom he admitted to be the chiefest adornment of earth. But the religion of the Bible, and especially of the New Testament, breathes a different spirit. Jesus found woman degraded, and stretched out his hand for her protection. When the severities of the Mosaic law were pointed out for his approval, he said, "In the beginning it was not so." He taught that "a man should leave father and mother and cleave unto his wife," thereby declaring that the relationship of marriage is the most sacred of all human ties. He taught what was a new revelation to the world, that all souls are equally precious in the sight of God; nor is there any thing more conspicuous in his history than the careful respect with which the women of the Gospel were treated. Wherever his religion is received, its first influence is to elevate her and defend her from oppression.

We might enlarge indefinitely upon these

topics; but more than enough has been said to show that every woman is bound, by her self-respect and by her desire for the respect of others, by the principles of her nature and by her social interests, by her own sense of duty and by allegiance to her sex, to devote herself, heart, soul, mind, and strength, to promote the cause of true religion and pure morality. Thus will she best work for the glory of God, and at the same time most effectually elevate herself to the place in society for which God designed her. It may be well enough for her, if she has a fancy for it, to declaim about her rights, and to hold conventions for the removal of her civil disabilities; for we do not deny that she has had in time past, or that she has now, many causes of just complaint. But the wrong can be made right, not by altering here and there a law, but only by the progress of true civilization. As men become better and wiser and more religious, woman will have continually less cause of complaint.

It was my intention to speak in this discourse of woman's duties towards the poor and suffering; but I have said so much on other topics, that I can say nothing on this. It is an important subject, which has never been treated as carefully as it deserves. The poor will never be properly provided for until they are placed more directly under woman's care. Poor-laws, almshouses, and committees of men are useful in their place, but charity is doubly blest when administered by woman's hand. Let her have the opportunity of learning by experience, so as to avoid being betrayed by her sympathies or by well-contrived imposture into injudicious action, and the same money will do more good and go further in her hands than in any other way. But I should incur the risk of tiring your patience, already too severely taxed, if I were to enlarge upon the subject now, and hope that at some future time I may find an opportunity of bringing it before you.

Here, then, is the true idea of woman's mission. In her own place, wherever it may be, and with all her influence, whether it seem to be great or little, let her count herself as the missionary of Christ's religion, a laborer with him in the cause of righteousness. Let her light so shine before men, that they, seeing her good works, may glorify the Father who is in heaven. Let her become the salt of the earth, remembering also, that if the salt lose its savor, the purifying influence of religion, it becomes more worthless even than common dust. I know that this is man's mission too, and that his life also becomes debased, unless consecrated to goodness. But woman is bound to the same cause by peculiar motives, and is able to prosecute it under peculiar advantages. She is able to begin at the beginning, to direct the first development of the mind, and almost to secure its growth in righteousness. She controls the affections of men, and thereby moulds their character. If she could only understand the importance of her position and the greatness of her work, as the educator of the human race, she would find enough to employ all her faculties, and to satisfy her highest ambition. Society has no other hope than this; for if woman becomes worldly and irreligious, society is educated in the same spirit, and its tendency must be continually downward.

In view of such great responsibility resting on her, have we not a right to demand of society, that greater means for woman's education should be provided? The education of the young is exclusively in her hands, and her natural capacity of teaching is greater than man's, so that the schools of our whole land are likely to be under her control; yet the provision for her own education is so imperfect, that she requires an unusual degree of diligence to become a well-educated person. In this respect society seems blind to its own interests. Legislators experiment in law-making, and incur the risk of dividing families by making a separate purse between husband and wife and by granting every facility of divorce, — experiments at which I cannot help looking with a good deal of distrust; but they do comparatively little to elevate the standard of woman's education. A state is seldom ten years old, perhaps not passed from the leading-strings of territorial government, before it has colleges and universities and high schools for boys and young men; but for females, the village school, with or without a beggarly appropriation, is accounted enough. But legislators do as their constituents demand, and the blame therefore rests where the punishment is felt; for the consequence is that women are but half-educated, and their duty as mothers and teachers but half performed.

Nor does the neglect cease with the school days. The whole arrangements of society, even in the most advanced cities of the world, seem to indicate that it is not expected of women to read or think, but that, as a general thing, it is enough, after her routine of duties is over, to enjoy herself and be agreeable.

We have lately seen in the newspapers descriptions of magnificent hotels in Eastern cities, built and furnished at a cost beyond that of palaces; and among the arrangements we find every appliance of luxury and elegance. For gentlemen, a reading-room is supplied with newspapers and journals from every part of the world, and with every facility for using them. But for ladies, Turkey carpets and silk curtains are enough, and neither book nor journal nor newspaper is provided for their use. Would it not be a popular, as it would certainly be a judicious movement, to provide a reading parlor or circulating library, together with other luxuries?

Care enough is taken of woman's comfort, but it would be well to think more of the intellectual enjoyment, and not compel her to resort to gossip or shopping, for the sake of passing the time.

In our library associations, also, which adorn every city and will soon become the pride of ours, how small encouragement is given, except to men, for their use! The lady may visit them as a matter of curiosity or for the selection of a book, but no place is assigned to her, where she can feel at home, for the purpose of reading books which she may not wish to take away, or where she may be quite sure that she is not intruding. I think that she should have equal rights and privileges in all such institutions. Give her the facilities of continued self-education and she will probably use them. Nearly all of us, whether men or women, conform ourselves, in a great degree, to what is expected of us. Let society expect and require of the young lady to be fond of reading and diligent in self-culture, and she will probably be glad to become so.

But after all the aids that society can give, the work of moral and intellectual improvement is chiefly in our own hands. It is a work of self-culture more than any thing else. The Scriptures teach that even our salvation must be worked out, under Divine direction, for ourselves. The same is true of education in knowledge and virtue, in the present life. The young must take hold of it with an individual purpose. They should use the means within their reach to the best advantage, and they will find that small opportunities well improved are better than the greatest if used less carefully. Let me end, therefore, as I began, in urging upon them the necessity of thoughtfulness and industry. Let the young lady determine that she will not be a trifler, devoted to pleasure, desiring only to be waited on, greedy of admiration, driven to and fro by every wind of fashion. Let her be at least as careful in the adorning of her mind as of her person. Let her have principles of conduct, from which neither the example nor persuasions of thoughtless people can make her swerve. However highly she may prize the elegances of life, let her prize still more highly the substance of life, which is found in modesty and a well-governed temper; in gentleness of manners and a womanly character. Some may smile at the homeliness of my advice, and they may find a more attractive and easier way in the routine of fashionable life. They may say that they have no particular desire to be wise and well-instructed, judicious and good women, and that they are satisfied to enjoy themselves as they go along. Their conduct proves the sincerity of their words, but they will probably live to see the day when all their fascinations will not save them from neglect, and the real trials of life will prove the necessity of real strength of character.

Finally, let the foundation of character be laid where alone it can be well laid, in religion. "Remember thy Creator in the days of thy youth." Hold fast to that religion which has redeemed your sex from servitude and degradation, and which is needed to redeem your own souls from the servitude of the world and the degradation of a selfish heart. Be religious; not sectarian or bigoted, as if the riches of God's grace were confined within the limits of this or that church; nor with a sentimental piety, very devout on Sunday and very worldly through the week; but be religious with genuine, sincere faith, with humility towards God and charity towards man.

Learn to be followers of Jesus Christ, who first understood the depths of woman's nature, and whose religion bestows upon her a strength which is not her own.

THE END.

www.ingramcontent.com/pod-product-compliance
Lightning Source LLC
LaVergne TN
LVHW011219110826
845150LV00006B/1476

* 9 7 8 1 4 2 5 5 1 6 1 0 9 *